Clarifying Your Missional Focus

Foundational Realities For Gospel Efforts

Darrell Leon Horn

Clarifying Your Missional Focus
Foundational Realities for Great Commission Efforts

Published by Darrell Leon Horn
Printed in the United States of America

ISBN: 0692160411
ISBN-13: 978-0692160411

Finally, brethren, pray for us that the word of the Lord will spread rapidly and be glorified, just as it did also with you.

2 Thessalonians 3:1

TABLE OF CONTENTS

THE MATTHEW AFFAIR

The Matthew Affair is a 501c3 non-profit organization dedicated to teaching and training the underserved. One primary focus is to teach and train underserved Christian pastors and leaders. It is estimated that up to 62% of the Christian Pastors around the world have not received any theological training.[1] We exist to serve them and anyone else who is underserved.

The author of this book receives no financial compensation. All proceeds from the sale of this book will be used by The Matthew Affair to achieve our stated purpose: to teach and train the underserved.

Tax exempt donations can be made at our website:
themattheweaffair.com

[1] "Up to 62 percent of the world's pastors have no formal training. There is an estimated 3.2M pastors in developing nations who have no Bible training." www.globalaction.com/glomos

IF EVERYTHING IS MISSIONS THEN NOTHING IS MISSIONS

Decline in GC Education

A decline in Great Commission education within local churches over the last several decades has produced believers who have a limited understanding of biblical missions. Such a decline has also produced believers who do not understand the panoramic view of God's self-revelation from eternity past to eternity future.[2] We are now dealing with,

---

[2] Chronological Bible Storytelling is a great method used to teach the progression of God's self-revelation to mankind in the order in which God chose to disclose Himself. The CBS method presents Bible stories in a chronological sequence with the intention of allowing the listener to connect the stories together for the purpose of forming a frame of reference of how God has revealed Himself to mankind. Old Testament stories are connected together to form the basis of understanding of why Christ's death, burial and resurrection were necessary in God's plan of

and have dealt with in the recent past, the results of a lack of proper teaching on the Great Commission. There are specific examples of such Great Commission education taking place but it is rather isolated while the majority of churches do not emphasize or provide such training.

The Barna Group[3] and the Seed Company[4] produced a study in 2018 concerning "the U.S. Church's ideas about missions, social justice, Bible translation and other aspects of spreading the gospel around the world."[5] The study was very revealing as well as troubling. The research exposed the following

> When asked if they had previously "heard of the Great Commission," half of U.S. churchgoers (51%) say they do not know this term. It would be

---

redemption.

[3] Barna Group is a private, non-partisan, for-profit organization under the umbrella of the Issachar Companies, which conducts and analyzes primary research to understand cultural trends related to values, beliefs, attitudes and behaviors.

[4] The Seed Company stated vision is: Our VISION for the next 10 years is to reach ONE BILLION more with God's Word! https://theseedcompany.org/about

[5] Barna Group, *Translating the Great Commission: What Spreading the Gospel Means to U.S. Christians in the 21st Century* (California: Barna Group, 2018). www.barna.com/research/half-churchgoers-not-heard-great-commission

reassuring to assume that the other half who know the term are also actually familiar with the passage known by this name, but that proportion is low (17%). Meanwhile, "the Great Commission" does ring a bell for one in four (25%), though they can't remember what it is. Six percent of churchgoers are simply not sure whether they have heard this term "the Great Commission" before.[6]

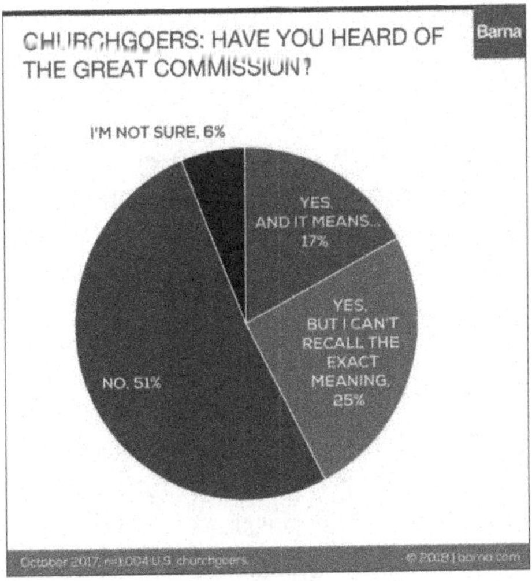

[7]

51 percent is a staggering number. The study does seem to indicate that certain denominations mention the Great Commission more than others in sermons and direct teaching. The study reveals

[6] Ibid.
[7] Ibid. Used by permission from the Barna Group.

> 28 percent of Southern Baptist pastors and 18 percent of Baptist pastors say their last sermon about missions was specifically about the Great Commission. Non-mainline pastors are typically more likely than mainline ministers to mention the Great Commission in a missions sermon (15% vs. 6%). In other words, the degree to which an individual churchgoer is personally aware of the phrasing of the Great Commission could be explained by the degree to which their own church denomination or leader publicly references it.[8]

The Great Commission is stated in at least 5 passages in the New Testament. More attention will be given to their similarities and differences in another section. The five places the Great Commission is given are: Matthew 28:18-20; Mark 16:15; Luke 24:45-47; John 20:21; and Acts 1:8. Barna found that

> Nearly all of the churchgoers who indicate they have previously heard of the Great Commission (94%) also select the passage in Matthew 28. The remainder of churchgoers either does not know which of these verses is the Great Commission (33%) or offers an incorrect answer (31%).

Some groups of churchgoers will typically have the opportunity to hear the Great Commission identified specifically or at least referenced in connection with mission sermons. One group of such churchgoers are

---

[8] Ibid.

the Baptists. Particularly Southern Baptist pastors (28%) and Baptist pastors (18%) indicate their last missions sermon about missions was about the Great Commission. Additional findings signify that the level of an individual's awareness of the phrase "the Great Commission" might "be explained by the degree to which their own church denomination or leader publicly references it."[9]

Here are some of the results of the study concerning which passages are recognizable.

DO CHURCHGOERS RECOGNIZE THE GREAT COMMISSION AMONG OTHER VERSES?	Barna
"Go and make disciples of all nations, baptizing them in the name of the Father and of the Son and of the Holy Spirit, and teaching them to obey everything I have commanded you." (Matthew 28:18-20)	37%
"'Love the Lord your God with all your heart and with all your soul with all your mind,' This is the first and greatest commandment. And the second is like it: 'Love your neighbor as yourself.'" (Matthew 22:37-40)	16%
"I am the way and the truth and the life. No one comes to the Father except through me." (John 14:6)	8%
"Whoever wants to be my disciple must deny themselves and take up their cross and follow me." (Mark 8:34)	5%
"Give back to Caesar what is Caesar's and to God what is God's." (Mark 12:17)	2%
Not sure if any of these passages are the Great Commission	33%
October 2017, n=1,004 U.S. churchgoers	© 2018 | barna.com

[10]

[9] Ibid.
[10] Ibid. Used by permission from the Barna Group.

This study sheds light on the troubling reality that we are facing – many decades of a lack of proper education in the local church on Christ's command to make disciples of all people groups. Such education includes but is not limited to cross cultural training, anthropological basics for using culture as a tool, chronological Bible storytelling, mission principles and philosophy, strategy and master plan training and development, people group studies, and language learning.

The argument could be made that nothing has changed from one generation to another and that what the study has disclosed is the normal state of things. Maybe so. Yet, there are many distinct examples to the contrary, suggesting that for many decades denominational churches have clearly moved away from Great Commission education. This reality is supported by the Barna study, which identified that

> roughly two in five people among the three oldest generations correctly identify the Great Commission (43% of Elders, 42% of Boomers, 41% of Gen X). Churchgoing Millennials, however, are about as likely to misidentify (36%) as to correctly identify (34%) the Great Commission.[11]

---

[11] Ibid.

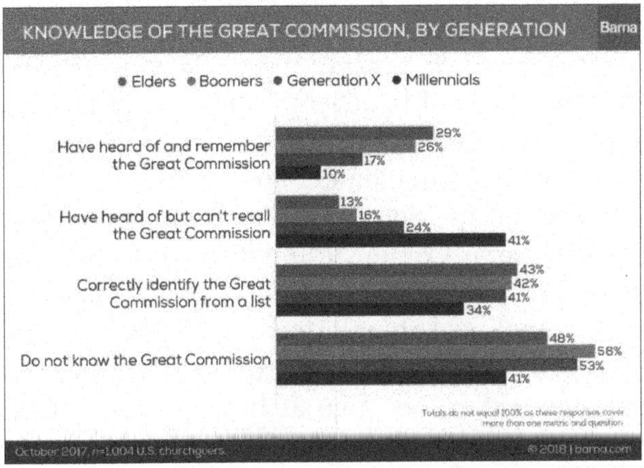

[12]

The evidence assembled illustrates that the expression "Great Commission" is being used less. This seems to be an indication that churches are giving less of a priority to the command of Christ or possibly that the phrase "the Great Commission" may have merely dropped out of preference.[13]

The study revealed an unknown factor in that it could not "conclude whether respondents are ignorant of the scriptural mandate itself, or just unaware that it is commonly called the Great Commission."[14]

---

[12] Ibid. Used by permission from the Barna Group.
[13] Ibid.
[14] Ibid.

If Everything Is Missions Then Nothing Is Missions

The vast majority of believers do not understand the difference between the Great Commission and the Second Great Commandment and could not name at least one basic mission principle. One evidence of our lack of Great Commission education in our local churches is the acceptance of the belief that everything the local church does outside its four walls is "missions." In fact, many churches believe being mission-minded is the same as being mission-active. To be mission-minded is to pray for mission activities and missionaries, take up offerings to support mission activities and missionaries, have "mission moments" during Sunday School, small groups and worship services, to have guest missionary speakers, as well as many other supportive efforts. To be mission-active is to send groups and individuals for personal hands-on involvement in mission activities. There is a tremendous need for churches that are both mission-minded and mission-active. Even within those churches that are mission-active, there is a belief that every activity is "missions."

The statement *"if everything is missions then nothing is missions"* is not new. Most of us have heard it many times. For quite some time the general understanding of the Great Commission has included a myriad of things such as humanitarian efforts, environmental issues, construction projects as well as many other topics and efforts. This broader list of items has also included such things as feeding programs, food pantries, quilting blankets for orphans, shoe collections, painting a widow's house, construction repairs and countless other activities. We have come to accept the broader definition of the Great Commission as *"everything we do is missions"* because of the decline in Great Commission education in the local church. The above statement is intended to challenge our beliefs about the Great Commission. If everything we do is considered a "mission" effort as from the Great Commission, then nothing we do is "missions."

Mission Misunderstood

How many times have you heard about a church or individual going on a "mission" trip? What made that trip a "mission" trip? What is the difference between that trip and any other trip? And what would make one more of a "mission" trip than another?

Here are a few examples. You can decide if these experiences are "mission" focused or not. Some time back I sat through a Mission Team presentation while visiting a Sunday morning worship service in a different part of my state. That particular Sunday morning just happened to be the worship service in which the church's "Mission Team" was giving a report from their weeklong trip to a South American country. The Mission Team Leader spoke about the main activity of the trip – going door-to-door collecting used cooking grease from the families who lived in a specific target neighborhood. This "begging for grease" activity gave the team an opportunity to meet each family in the neighborhood where the host church was located. Sounds good, right? It allowed the team members to meet the neighborhood families.

What did the team do with the grease? As I listened to the presentation I asked myself the same question. The team took the used cooking grease and made soap out of it. The team explained the multi-day process that was used to turn the grease into soap. Somewhere around the fourth day, the team returned to each home that had donated the grease and gave each family the soap that had been made that week. The team leader and team members mentioned no other activity that was accomplished on the trip.

Was that a "mission" trip? Why or why not?

After listening to the "grease to soap" story, I kept waiting to hear how the Gospel was presented to the families receiving the soap, or how someone heard the Gospel and then gave his or her life to Christ. However, based on what was presented, soap making was the main activity of the trip.

Would you consider that trip to be a "mission" trip or another type of trip? You might be thinking, yea but that is an unusual example. None of us would consider that a mission trip. Yet, the missions pastor and his church were excited about the trip and the fact that they were doing "missions" in a foreign country.

Back to the original statement, if everything we do is considered missions then we have blurred the lines so much as to what missions really is, that everything we do becomes "missions." The trip to South America was clearly not a mission trip. In fact, I'm not sure what type of trip I would label it but that trip was not a "missions" trip. The question remains, What makes any trip a "mission" trip?

Here is another example of a church calling everything "missions." The pastor of an established church in a southern state in the United States was friends with a pastor starting a new church in the northeastern part of the United States. The pastor of the established church formed a volunteer group of 15-18 members and traveled to the northeast where the new church was being started. The group of volunteers arrived and immediately began cleaning out the basement of the building where the new church was meeting. The team worked hard because the basement was extremely filthy. They worked so diligently that they were able to finish cleaning the building a day early. During the week a few members of the volunteer team would walk a number of blocks to a subway entrance. The team members carried bottles of water with informational labels about the new church. They stood at the entrance of the subway and passed out water to people on the street. They spoke to anyone walking by, when given the opportunity.

Upon returning from the trip, the pastor of the

established church shared with his congregation that the highlight of the trip was when a taxi driver asked for another bottle of "Jesus Juice." Obviously the "Jesus Juice" was in reference to the bottled water the team was handing out. The Gospel was not shared on the trip but several bottles of water were. What type of trip was this?

If we call everything we do "missions," then nothing we do is "missions." What about the trips that do construction projects? Or a trip focused on feeding programs or helping orphans? How do we distinguish what is "missions" and what is not? The next section will discuss a number of answers to those questions.

Key Concepts . . . .

- We are facing a troubling reality – many decades of a lack of proper education in the local church on Christ's command to make disciples of all people groups.
- A decline in Great Commission education within the local church over the last several decades has produced believers who have a limited understanding of biblical missions.
- 51 percent of churchgoers do not know the term "Great Commission."
- Evidence from the study illustrates that the term "Great Commission" is being used less.
- Most believers do not understand the difference between the Great Commission and the Second Great Commandment and could not name at least one basic mission principle.
- Being mission-minded and being mission-active are two distinct and separate things.
- If everything we do is considered a "mission" effort as from the Great Commission, then nothing we do is "missions."

¿-? Questions to consider . . . .

1. What in this chapter has challenged you?

2. How does your church compare to the Barna Group and The Seed Company report?

3. What changes might you need to make in your church or ministry to avoid such a decline?

4. Can you explain the difference between the Great Commission and the Second Great Commandment?

5. How many mission principles can you name?

6. What opportunities do you have in the near future to share the truths of this chapter with others?

The Great Commission

Introduction

Three mandates of the Church are: love God with all your heart, soul, mind and strength;[15] love your neighbor as you love yourself;[16] and make disciples of all people groups.[17] What is the difference between the Second Great Commandment to love your neighbor as yourself and the Great Commission to make disciples of all people groups?

The Great Commission and the Second Great Commandment are both necessary elements in a well-balanced approach to missions and ministry. Yet, there is a difference between the Great Commission and the Second Great Commandment. Most believers are unaware of this difference. Not understanding the difference is the main reason we typically call everything missions: from feeding

---

[15] Deuteronomy 6:5; Matthew 22:37
[16] Leviticus 19:18; Matthew 22:39
[17] Matthew 28:18-20

programs; food pantries; quilting blankets for orphans; shoe collections; painting a widow's house; construction repairs; and countless other activities.

"if everything is missions then nothing is missions"

We must understand the contrasts between the Great Commission to make disciples and the Second Great Commandment to love your neighbor as yourself. Both of these go together but they are distinctly different.

The Great Commission

The Great Commission is listed at least five times in the New Testament. Here are those five references:

Matthew 28:18-20 "And Jesus came up and spoke to them, saying, 'All authority has been given to Me in heaven and on earth. Go therefore and make disciples of all the nations, baptizing them in the name of the Father and the Son and the Holy Spirit, teaching them to observe all that I commanded you; and lo, I am with you always, even to the end of the age.'"

Mark 16:15 "And He said to them, 'Go into all the world and preach the Gospel to all creation.'"

Luke 24:45-47 "Then He opened their minds to understand the Scriptures, and He said to them, 'Thus it is written, that the Christ would suffer and rise again from the dead the third day, and that repentance for forgiveness of sins would be proclaimed in His name to all the nations, beginning from Jerusalem.'"

John 20:21 "So Jesus said to them again, 'Peace be with you; as the Father has sent Me, I also send you.'"

Acts 1:8 "but you will receive power when the Holy Spirit has come upon you; and you shall be My witnesses both in Jerusalem, and in all Judea and Samaria, and even to the remotest part of the earth."

There is an additional reference, which some might consider as an additional reference to the Great Commission, if not an actual example. 1 Corinthians 5:20 states, "Therefore, we are ambassadors for Christ, as though God were making an appeal through us; we beg you on behalf of Christ, be reconciled to God."

Each one of these declarations gives us a little more information concerning Christ's mandate. A simple comparison chart helps us better understand what Christ wants us to do, to communicate, to whom we communicate, and what additional actions need to be taken. The chart is shown below.

We are able to gain a better understanding of Christ's assignment to the Church as we look through the different ways in which the Great Commission is expressed in each passage. It is obvious that Christ is sending out His Church in His name with His power; the power of His Spirit enabling the message to penetrate the heart of those who hear.

Great Commission Chart

Passage	To Where	To Whom	To Be	Message Spoken	Actions Taken
Matthew 28:18-20	Where the "all nations" live	All nations	Disciplers Baptizers teachers	All things that Christ commanded	Make, baptize and teach disciples in the name of the Father, the Son and the Holy Spirit
Mark 16:15-16	All the world	All creation	Preachers	The Gospel	Preach
Luke 24:45-47	Beginning from Jerusalem then to where ever "all nations" live	All the nations	Proclaimers	That Christ would suffer and rise again from the dead the third day, and that repentance for forgiveness of sins would be proclaimed in His name	Proclaim the message in Christ's name
John 20:21					Be sent
Acts 1:8	Jerusalem Judea, Samaria, ends of the earth	Those who live in Jerusalem Judea, Samaria, and the ends of the earth	Witnesses	What you saw as a witness	Be witnesses
1 Cor 5:20			Ambassadors	Be reconciled to God	

In the Book of Acts, the Gospel was proclaimed and the Church grew through its obedience to the Great Commission in the decades following Christ's ascension. Acts 1:8 is the outline of the book of Acts: Jerusalem;[18] Judea;[19] Samaria;[20] and the ends of the earth are the various sections to the book.[21] Chapters 1 to 7 focus on the Church in Jerusalem while Judea is mentioned 13 times and is referenced throughout the book of Acts. Judea and Samaria are mentioned together only three times, Acts 1:8, 8:1 and 9:31. Samaria is primarily mentioned in chapter 8 when Phillip preaches there. Only two other references to Samaria exist in Acts, 9:31 and 15:3. Efforts to reach the ends of the earth begin with the commissioning of two missionaries in chapter 13, Barnabas and Paul. The majority, of the Acts narrative from chapters 13-28, are focused on Paul taking the Gospel to the Gentile people groups.

Paul And The Great Commission

As the Church grew so did persecution. Yet, in the midst of persecution, the Book of Acts records God drawing one person out from the crowd. It was a

[18] Jerusalem is mentioned 60 times in Acts from 1:4 to 28:17

[19] Acts 8:1; 9:31; 10:37; 11:1; 11:29; 12:19; 15:1; 21:10; 16:20; and 28:21

[20] Acts 1:8; 8:1, 4-5, 9, 14; 9:31; and 15:3

[21] Acts 13-28

young man named Paul, who held the crowd's garments and approved of the stoning of Stephen.[22] This young man later had an encounter with the risen Christ on the road to Damascus.[23] God called out Paul and transformed him. God later told Ananias to go and pray for Paul to regain his sight after his experience on the road to Damascus. God told Ananias that Paul was "a chosen instrument of Mine, to bear My name before the Gentiles and kings and the sons of Israel; for I will show him how much he must suffer for My name's sake."[24] God rose up an Apostle, named Paul, "as to one untimely born"[25] who became the great missionary of the New Testament and the Church of all ages.

Paul became a very influential missionary presence to the known world of that time. There were others who were called and sent out to the regions of the Roman Empire; Barnabas being one of them. Yet Paul is the one to whom Luke devotes the majority of his writings in the book of Acts. Luke faithfully records the acts of the Holy Spirit through Paul's efforts. Unquestionably, we consider Paul to be the greatest missionary, not only of the early Church but of all Church history. For that reason, Paul's missionary activities are considered to be the prime example of the fulfillment of the Great Commission. Paul sought to live out Christ's command and God's call on his

---

[22] Acts 7:58
[23] Acts 9:1-9
[24] Acts 9:15-16
[25] 1 Corinthians 15:8

life to bear His name to the Gentiles, kings and the sons of Israel. Paul told King Agrippa that he had been faithful to the heavenly vision,[26] which occurred as he was on his way to Damascus. Paul states the following to King Agrippa,

> I did not prove disobedient to the heavenly vision, but kept declaring both to those of Damascus first, and also at Jerusalem and then throughout all the region of Judea, and even to the Gentiles, that they should repent and turn to God, performing deeds appropriate to repentance.[27]

Again, we consider Paul's missionary activities to be a fulfillment of Christ's Commission to the Church. Paul's normal missionary activity included the following: preach the Gospel; gather the new believers as the local church; baptize the new believers; disciple the new believers (teaching them to observe all things); pray over the new believers dedicating them to the Lord; appoint elders in every city; leave the local church in order to repeat the process in the next area; and then visit the church again in the future and or write letters to that church.

The Book of Acts should be called "Acts of the Holy Spirit" instead of "Acts of the Apostles." It was the Spirit of God, which made possible the preaching of the Gospel to "all the nations" or people groups.

---

[26] Acts 9:1-9

[27] Acts 26:19-20

What is the Gospel? Paul uses the word "Gospel" when writing to the Corinthian church. He states, "Now I make known to you, brethren, the Gospel which I preached to you, which also you received, in which also you stand, by which also you are saved, if you hold fast the word which I preached to you, unless you believed in vain."[28] He explained the word "Gospel" when he wrote

> For I delivered to you as of first importance what I also received, that Christ died for our sins according to the Scriptures, and that He was buried, and that He was raised on the third day according to the Scriptures.[29]

The message is consistent with Jesus' statement in Luke 24, when He opened their minds to understand the Scriptures, and He said to them, "Thus it is written, that the Christ would suffer and rise again from the dead the third day, and that repentance for forgiveness of sins would be proclaimed in His name to all the nations, beginning from Jerusalem." The resurrection and the repentance for the forgiveness of sins in Christ's name is the Gospel message. This is the message that Paul preached on his missionary journeys.

We see in Acts 14 on their first missionary trip, Barnabas and Paul went to many cities preaching the Gospel. Luke states in verse 1, "In Iconium they

---

[28] 1 Corinthians 15:1-2

[29] 1 Corinthians 15:3-4

entered the synagogue of the Jews together, and spoke in such a manner that a large number of people believed, both of Jews and of Greeks." They preached the Gospel message and many believed. In verses 6 and 7 we see that Barnabas and Paul went to "the cities of Lycaonia, Lystra and Derbe, and the surrounding region; and there they continued to preach the Gospel." The following verses reveal the methodology that was used by Barnabas and Paul.

> After they had preached the Gospel to that city and had made many disciples, they returned to Lystra and to Iconium and to Antioch, strengthening the souls of the disciples, encouraging them to continue in the faith, and saying, "Through many tribulations we must enter the kingdom of God." When they had appointed elders for them in every church, having prayed with fasting, they commended them to the Lord in whom they had believed.[30]

The normal methodology employed by Barnabas and Paul was to preach the Gospel, to gather the new believers as the local church, to baptize the new believers, to disciple the new believers (teaching them to observe all things), to pray over the new believers dedicating them to the Lord, to appoint elders in every city, to leave the local church in order to repeat the process in the next area. Paul later wrote letters back to the churches he had planted and

---

[30] Acts 14:21-23

to some churches he had not.

The seeding of the Gospel, around the known world of Paul's day, was done by a non-dependent, indigenous and reproducible strategy. Paul consistently employed these three mission principles from city to city.

This is the main idea we need to take away from the Great Commission efforts in the book of Acts, because Paul is our example to follow in our activities Great Commission. What Paul did is our pattern for current day Great Commission efforts. Let me make that point again; what Paul did is our pattern for current day Great Commission efforts. This includes the previously stated activities such of preaching the Gospel, gathering the new believers as the local church, baptizing the new believers, discipling the new believers (teaching them to observe all things), praying over the new believers dedicating them to the Lord, appointing elders in every city, leaving the local church in order to repeat the process in the next area and then visiting again in the future and or writing letters to them.

We see this pattern repeated over and over in Paul's Great Commission efforts. In Acts 16, Paul, Silas, Timothy and Luke arrive in "Philippi, which is a leading city of the district of Macedonia, a Roman colony."[31] Luke states, "And on the Sabbath day we went outside the gate to a riverside, where we were

---

[31] Acts 16:12

supposing that there would be a place of prayer; and we sat down and began speaking to the women who had assembled."[32]

Paul proclaimed the Gospel and "a woman named Lydia, from the city of Thyatira, a seller of purple fabrics, a worshiper of God, was listening; and the Lord opened her heart to respond to the things spoken by Paul."[33] Obviously, others listening that day responded also. Luke tells us that Lydia and "her household" were baptized immediately. Later in the Philippian account, Paul and Silas encounter a jailer who becomes a believer and is baptized, along with his entire household. Luke states the jailer "rejoiced greatly, having believed in God with his whole household."[34] After Paul and Silas were released from prison, they "entered the house of Lydia, and when they saw the brethren, they encouraged them and departed."[35] Paul later wrote a letter to the church in Philippi. The inspired account of Acts 16 provides us with a background through which we are able to better understand the letter to the church in Philippi.

In Acts 17 Paul and Silas go to Thessalonica where they proclaimed, "This Jesus whom I proclaim to you is the Christ."[36] As they preached in the synagogue for

---

[32] Acts 16:13
[33] Acts 16:14
[34] Acts 16:34
[35] Acts 16:40
[36] Acts 17:3

three Sabbaths, "some of them were persuaded and joined Paul and Silas along with a great multitude of God-fearing Greeks and a number of the leading women."[37] Paul and his team of missionaries preached in Berea, Athens, Corinth, Macedonia, Ephesus, and Antioch, Galatian region, Phrygia, Achaia, and other places. Paul continued to fulfill the missionary call that God had placed on his life until the very end. Luke concludes the Book of Acts with this statement

> For two whole years Paul stayed there in his own rented house and welcomed all who came to see him. He proclaimed the kingdom of God and taught about the Lord Jesus Christ—with all boldness and without hindrance![38]

[37] Acts 17:4
[38] Acts 28:30-31

Key Concepts . . . .

Here are a number of observations concerning the fulfillment of the Great Commission in the Book of Acts. This is not an exhaustive list.

- Paul gave us a pattern to follow when "making disciples of all people groups."
- The Holy Spirit called missionaries from the local church to be sent out – Acts 13.
- Sent out missionaries do many activities as an extension of the sending church.
- If a local church did not exist then one was started. New believers need a spiritual home in which to grow - that spiritual home is a local church.
- The sending church and the new church started are both an integral part of Great Commission efforts.
- Great Commission efforts are never done apart from the local church.
- Evangelism is not enough – new believers must be gathered together for mutual spiritual support and continued spiritual growth.
- Great Commission efforts were essentially the same in every location: the Gospel was preached, new believers were gathered together as the local church, new believers were baptized, new believers were discipled, elders were appointed to lead the new church, and the new local church was dedicated to the Lord.
- New churches existed in each of the more than

40 cities named in the Book of Acts.

- Great Commission efforts result in new believers, new churches and new leaders.
- Great Commission efforts must not create dependency, must be indigenous to the local culture and must be reproducible.

¿-? Questions to consider . . . .

1. What in this chapter has challenged you?

2. What is the Great Commission?

3. How did Paul's life exemplify the Great Commission?

4. Can you explain the difference between the Great Commission and the Second Great Commandment?

5. How many mission principles can you name?

6. What opportunities do you have in the near future to share the truths of this chapter with others?

The Second Great Commandment

The Second Great Commandment appears first in Moses's writings when he stated the Lord commands, "You shall not take vengeance, nor bear any grudge against the sons of your people, but you shall love your neighbor as yourself; I am the Lord."[39] This foundational teaching is the basis for Christ's commands, as well as those of Paul. On one occasion, Jesus was asked by a scribe, "What commandment is the foremost of all?" Jesus responded by restating the two Great Commandments. "The foremost is, 'Hear, O Israel! The Lord our God is one Lord; and you shall love the Lord your God with all your heart, and with all your soul, and with all your mind, and with all your strength.' The second is this, 'You shall love your neighbor as yourself.' There is no other

[39] Leviticus 19:18

commandment greater than these."[40] Jesus also stated, "A new commandment I give to you, that you love one another, even as I have loved you, that you also love one another. By this all men will know that you are My disciples, if you have love for one another."[41] Jesus mentions an act of kindness even as small as giving a cup of water will have a reward. He stated, "And whoever in the name of a disciple gives to one of these little ones even a cup of cold water to drink, truly I say to you, he shall not lose his reward."[42]

In the Scriptures, it is Christ who gives us the most clarity on this commandment. There are no other passages, except from the Gospels, which interpret so clearly the Leviticus verse. For example, one day when Jesus was teaching and answering questions, a lawyer, who wanted to put Jesus to the test, asked him "Who is my neighbor?" So Jesus told the story of the Good Samaritan. What a story to illustrate the command to love your neighbor as yourself. Instead of discussing the issue with one point after another, Jesus gives his answer in such a way that it is impossible to misunderstand what he is saying. The Samaritan was despised by the Jews yet Jesus makes him the hero of the story. Jesus touches Jewish emotions and taboos with His story and His point cuts to the quick.

---

[40] Mark 12:29-31
[41] John 13:34-35
[42] Matthew 10:42

There are many other passages in the New Testament which speak of this commandment. When Paul wrote to the church in Galatia, he stated, "For the whole Law is fulfilled in one word, in the statement, 'You shall love your neighbor as yourself.'"[43] Again when writing to the church in Rome, Paul states, "and if there is any other commandment, it is summed up in this saying, 'You shall love your neighbor as yourself.' Love does no wrong to a neighbor; therefore love is the fulfillment of the law."[44]

"James, the Lord's brother"[45][46] stated that we do well if we fulfill "the royal law according to the Scripture, 'You shall love your neighbor as yourself.'"[47] God is please by His Church meeting human needs and demonstrating kindness and respect to those less fortunate. James does remind us that "if you show partiality, you are committing sin *and* are convicted by the law as transgressors."[48] Again, God is involved when kindness and generosity are extended to others.

---

[43] Galatians 5:14

[44] Romans 13:9-10

[45] Galatians 1:19

[46] James was the half brother of Jesus. At one time he and his kinsman did not believe what Jesus was teaching. They thought Jesus had "lost His senses." Mark 3:21. After Jesus' resurrection, James eventually became the lead elder in the Jerusalem church and is seen in Acts 15. Paul visited him on one of his trips to Jerusalem in Galatians 1:18-19 and Acts 21:18.

[47] James 2:8

[48] James 2:9

Proverbs teaches us that the "One who is gracious to a poor man lends to the Lord, And He will repay him for his good deed."[49]

In the Book of Acts, the Apostles continue to follow the example that Christ had set for them. As "Peter and John were going up to the temple at the ninth hour, the hour of prayer,"[50] a man, lame from birth, was begging for alms. Peter tells him,

> I do not possess silver and gold, but what I do have I give to you: "In the name of Jesus Christ the Nazarene—walk!" And seizing him by the right hand, he raised him up; and immediately his feet and his ankles were strengthened. With a leap he stood upright and began to walk; and he entered the temple with them, walking and leaping and praising God.[51]

Peter then uses the occasion, meeting a human need, to communicate the Gospel message when he delivered his second sermon recorded in the Book of Acts.

The Second Great Commandment is to: love your neighbor as yourself;[52] feed the hungry;[53] cloth the

---

[49] Proverbs 19:17
[50] Acts 3:1
[51] Acts 3:6-8
[52] Matthew 19:19
[53] Matthew 25:35

naked;[54] visit those in prison;[55] care for widows and orphans;[56] heal the sick;[57] and entertain strangers;[58] give a cup of cold water;[59] and help the poor.[60] Meeting human needs shows compassion and honors God.

[54] Matthew 25:36; James 2:15-16
[55] Matthew 25:36
[56] James 1:27
[57] Matthew 14:14
[58] Matthew 25:35; Hebrew 13:2
[59] Matthew 10:42
[60] Proverbs 19:17

Key Concepts . . . .

- The Second Great Commandment first appears in Leviticus 19:18.
- Jesus confirms the two Great Commandments: "The foremost is, 'Hear, O Israel! The Lord our God is one Lord; and you shall love the Lord your God with all your heart, and with all your soul, and with all your mind, and with all your strength.' The second is this, 'You shall love your neighbor as yourself.' There is no other commandment greater than these."
- We demonstrate the Second Great Commandment, to love your neighbor as yourself, when we feed the hungry, cloth the naked, visit those in prison, care for widows and orphans, heal the sick, entertain strangers and help the poor.
- Meeting human needs shows compassion and honors God.

¿-? Questions to consider . . . .

1. What in this chapter has challenged you?

2. What is the Second Great Commandment?

3. What did Jesus, Paul and the Scriptures teach us about the Second Great Commandment?

4. What opportunities do you have in the near future to share the truths of this chapter with others?

Commission and Commandment Together

In order to have a better understanding of what mission is, it is important to look both at the Great Commission and the Second Great Commandment simultaneously. The following is a quick review of the previous two chapters. In essence, the Great Commission, as witnessed in the Book of Acts, is to preach the Gospel, to gather the new believers as the local church, to baptize new believers, to disciple the new believers to observe everything Christ commanded them, to pray over the new believers dedicating them to the Lord, to appoint elders in every city, to leave the local church in order to repeat the process in the next area to receive the Gospel message. While an expression of the Second Great Commandment is to love your neighbor as yourself, is to feed the hungry, to cloth the naked, to visit those in prison, to care for widows and orphans, to heal the sick, and to entertain strangers.

What the modern day church calls "missions" has

often been associated with meeting human needs such as humanitarian aid and social ministries while assuming that by meeting those needs the Gospel has been preached. The phrase, "Preach the gospel at all times. Use words if necessary," has been attributed to Francis of Assisi even though he did not make the comment.[61] This well-known phrase implies that the Gospel can be preached only by our actions. This is a false assumption. When the Gospel was communicated in Scripture it was done so through teaching and preaching.

What the modern day church calls the Great Commission, meeting human needs, is a misunderstanding of the Great Commission. Meeting human needs is an expression of the Second Great Commandment and not the Great Commission. This misunderstanding has led many to believe that everything we do outside the four walls of the church building is a Great Commission activity. Some leaders have indicated that understanding the difference does not make any impact at all on what we do. Such a statement shows the depth to which our decline in proper Great Commission education has fallen.

The goal of a balanced mission and ministry is to do both things without the omission of the other. Christ

---

[61] Midwest Capuchin Franciscans Vocation – www.capuchinfranciscans.org/blog/preach-the-gospel-at-all-times-if-necessary-use-words

is our example. He did both at the same time. Matthew identifies Christ's work in Galilee as "teaching in their synagogues and proclaiming the gospel of the kingdom, and healing every kind of disease and every kind of sickness among the people."[62] He proclaimed the Gospel and then met human needs. When He saw "the people, He felt compassion for them, because they were distressed and dispirited like sheep without a shepherd. Then He said to His disciples, "The harvest is plentiful, but the workers are few. Therefore beseech the Lord of the harvest to send out workers into His harvest."[63] Matthew, on another occasion, states that not only in Galilee but "through all the cities and villages" Jesus was "teaching in their synagogues and proclaiming the gospel of the kingdom, and healing every kind of disease and every kind of sickness."[64] Obviously, this was a common aspect of his ministry.

One day a disciple of John came to Jesus and asked if he was the "Expected One." Jesus' answer includes both the Great Commandment and the Great Commission. Jesus stated

> Go and report to John what you hear and see: the blind receive sight and the lame walk, the lepers are cleansed and the deaf hear, the dead are raised up, and the poor have

---

[62] Matthew 4:23
[63] Matthew 9:36-38
[64] Matthew 9:35

the gospel preached to them.[65]

Both are necessary components of the meeting the whole needs of people. However, just because one component is present does not mean the other one is also. Many people will share the Gospel and not attempt to meet the human needs of others while some only meet human needs and do not share the Gospel. To meet human needs without including a presentation of the Gospel is like working for the Peace Corps.[66] If someone wants to meet human needs only, then the Peace Corps is a great place. But within a Christian context, the Gospel must be included. We can meet all the human needs that exist but if we do not include the Gospel, then those who receive our help will pass into a Christ-less eternity. Just because you are physically present meeting human needs does not mean the Gospel is communicated. Once again, we can meet every human need that exists and people, without Christ, will still pass into eternity unprepared to face the judgment to come.

The presence of the a believer does not means the Gospel is being proclaimed

---

[65] Matthew 11:4-5

[66] The Peace Corps is a service opportunity for motivated changemakers to immerse themselves in a community abroad, working side by side with local leaders to tackle the most pressing challenges of our generation. https://www.peacecorps.gov/about

The misunderstanding of calling everything we do missions or of only meeting human needs is like trying to fly an airplane with only one wing. Two wings are needed to balance the plane. So, two foci are needed to balance the efforts of the Church.

Donald McGavran[67] precisely identifies the pitfall of a secondary aim such as meeting human needs becoming main focus of our efforts while making disciples of all people groups takes a back seat. McGavran states

> It is virtually impossible to participate in the missionary task without incorporating biblically based Christian ministry. However, participation in effective biblically based Christian ministry can be provided without ever crossing the line into missions. As a result of the small response in new mission work they were easily diverted to *secondary aims*. Not only did the missions turn to *secondary aims* but they came to consider them *primary*. The sending Boards and churches made no distinction between mission enterprises serving the *primary aim* and those serving the *secondary*

[67] "McGavran was born in Damoh, India, in 1897. As a third-generation missionary, McGavran's family totaled 279 years of service in India by 1954. Donald McGavran credited his early missionary training and experience to the friendship and guidance of his father, John McGavran."
https://en.wikipedia.org/wiki/Donald_McGavran

> *aims.*[68]

McGavran's observation comes from his missionary experience in India. His point is well taken and quite clear. When we become so focused on a secondary activity, such as only meeting human needs, it will eventually replace our primary focus of making disciples of all people groups. The secondary will replace the primary and will cause the primary focus to become secondary. The Gospel is primary while the meeting of human needs is the secondary focus.

Gerald Harris also correctly identifies the proper balance between the Great Commission and the Great commandment. He writes

> The social gospel embraces ministries that provide help to the needy – clothes closets, food banks, and health-clinics – almost anything that would contribute to the welfare of society. Churches should be engaged in these social ministries, but these ministries should not be the primary objective. Every social ministry or act of kindness should create a bridge to share the Gospel. When I was pastor of Eastside Baptist Church in Marietta I read Steve Sjogren's book *Conspiracy of Kindness.* Sjogren gives his readers an almost unlimited list of unassuming acts of kindness that Christians can practice to communicate the love of Christ. I discovered that

[68] Donald McGavran. *Bridges of God.*

many of our folks were excited about giving out water on a hot summer day, painting house numbers on the edge of the sidewalk, shining people's shoes for free in the mall, and even providing free gift wrapping for a department store at Christmas, but they never shared the Gospel. Good deeds are important, but there are countless service organizations that help the public. Christians not only have the privilege of putting a man in a new suit, but putting a new man in a suit as a result of the change wrought by sharing the Gospel.[69]

[69] Gerald Harris. *The Southern Baptist Convention is Undergoing a Seismic Shift.* Christian Index. https://christianindex.org/the-southern-baptist-convention-is-undergoing-a-seismic-shift/

Key Concepts . . . .

- Groups, churches or individuals from outside the geographical target area should work with local existing churches and or missionaries (especially if there is no local church) so the results of Gospel efforts can be sustained after the groups, churches or individuals have gone
- It is the responsibility of the local church to meet the existing human needs and make disciples of its own community
- The local church should lead any efforts to meet human needs and share the Gospel
- All believers need a spiritual home in which to grow and mature. The local church is that spiritual home. If a local church does not exist, start one
- We can feed everyone who is hungry, cloth everyone who is naked, build shelters for the homeless, heal everyone who is sick, and visit everyone in prison, but if we do not lead individuals into a saving relationship with Jesus Christ, they die spending eternity separated from Christ
- When we become so concentrated on a secondary ministry, such as only meeting human needs, the secondary ministry will eventually replace our primary focus of making disciples of all people groups
- The Gospel is primary while the meeting of human needs is the secondary focus and provide opportunities to the primary

- We must have a balanced approach to missions and ministry

Mandates of the Church

Love the Lord your God with all your heart and with all your soul and with all your might. You shall love your neighbor as yourself	Great Commandment (MINISTRY)
Go make disciples Baptize them Teach them	Great Commission (MISSIONS)

¿-? Questions to consider . . . .

1. What in this chapter has challenged you?

2. Can you explain the difference between the Great Commission and the Second Great Commandment?

3. How do the Great Commission and the Great Commandment complement each other?

4. What happens when meeting human needs is primary and the Great Commission is secondary?

5. What opportunities do you have in the near future to share the truths of this chapter with others?

Three Vital Principles

There are several basis missiological principles by which all missions and ministry should function. The word "missiology" is the study of God's mission – missio dei. Missiological principles are discovered as God's mission is expressed through the Church. Principles are foundational or fundamental truths that are valid for any historical era, any cultural context, any linguistic setting, and any individual or group seeking to apply them. As we study the history of the Church we are able to identify the types of Gospel efforts God has blessed and those He has not. Missiological principles are those macro truths that transcend any culture, language or time in history.

We are able to avoid many pitfalls in mission and ministry work when we are guided by such basic principles. Many well-intentioned individuals and groups serve God with a sincere heart yet employ methods in their mission and or ministry activities that actually hinder or stop the spread of the Gospel.

In other words, the methods used were counter-productive to the intended goal of the mission and or ministry activity. There are times when we do more harm than good to the spread of the Gospel because of the methods we use.

Paul requested prayer from the church in Thessalonica when he stated, "Finally, brethren, pray for us that the Word of the Lord will spread rapidly and be glorified, just as it did also with you."[70] Paul saw the importance of the Word of God being unhindered in order to spread rapidly. It is vital that we employ methodologies that meet these three basic requirements. We should rethink the methodologies we employ and filter our activities through the N. I. R. Missiological Principles. We should become NEAR sighted (N. I. R.) when it comes to understanding missiological principles. The N. I. R. Missiological Principles are: **N**on-dependency; **I**ndigeneity; and **R**eproducibility. The following chapters provide a more in-depth explanation of these indispensible foundations of good missions and ministry, including several examples of all three principles.

[70] 2 Thessalonians 3:1

Non-Dependency

Dependency is an important issue to consider when we evaluate the "how" and the "why" we do what we do in missions and ministry. Sincerity of heart toward God is not the issue here – correct methodology is. We can be sincere in what we are seeking to accomplish and have pure motives but yet use methods that hinder the spread of the Gospel. Improper methods do not create the outcomes we desire. Dependency is created when we teach others to depend on us instead of teaching them to rely on God and themselves. We create dependency, directly or indirectly, anytime we instruct others rely on us. This occurs not always through our direct words but through our actions and attitudes. For example, there are appropriate situations in which we share resources but under certain conditions. We want to create partners in ministry and missions not dependents.

Dependency enervates, which means to deprive of force or strength and to destroy the vigor of something.[71] Some of the methods we use in missions and ministry actually create an environment that stifles growth and harms our long-term efforts. Dependency handicaps and hinders the process of spiritual maturation by creating a welfare mentality. When considering a well-balanced missions and ministry approach, we must take a serious look at two non-dependency guidelines.

We do not do for others what they can already do for themselves.

We create an unhealthy environment by doing missions and ministry activities for others when they are capable of doing it themselves. We teach others to depend on us and not on God by doing for them what they can and should already be doing for themselves. This type of mindset is demonstrated when an individual or a group relies on others for outside assistance and they do not plan to stop.

There is a clear distinction between a hand-out and a hand-up. Giving aid to someone in need honors Christ. Yet continually enabling someone to live a spiritual life of reliance on others does not. We should expect all believers to take responsibility for their own spiritual development and not remain babes in Christ. We should expect all believers to

[71] https://www.dictionary.com/browse/enervate

invest in their own spiritual development. To not expect such spiritual commitment is to allow others to remain undisciplined in their own maturation. This was true in the life of Paul. He stated in his letter to the Corinth church,

> And I, brethren, could not speak to you as to spiritual men, but as to men of flesh, as to infants in Christ. I gave you milk to drink, not solid food; for you were not yet able to receive it. Indeed, even now you are not yet able, for you are still fleshly. For since there is jealousy and strife among you, are you not fleshly, and are you not walking like mere men?[72]

This type of mentality debilitates others and creates a spiritual welfare mindset. Such misguided relationships create dependents not disciples. If we are to take serious Paul's instructions to Timothy, we must use methods that produce disciples not dependents. Paul told Timothy, "The things, which you have heard from me in the presence of many witnesses, entrust these to faithful men who will be able to teach others also."[73] Four generations of disciples can be identified in this one verse: Paul; Timothy; faithful men; others. This fact will be expounded in the "*Reproducibility*" section.

We must take a sober look at this fact. Based on the methods we use and what we expect from others,

[72] 1 Corinthians 3:1-3
[73] 2 Timothy 2:2

what type of disciples are we creating? We must allow and even expect others to do for themselves what they can and should be doing already. Many times we continue the ministry of propping up others spiritually when they should be seeking to grow on their own by practicing the things they already know. Unfortunately, at times we don't expect others to take personal responsibility for their own growth and allow them to remain in spiritual infancy because we do too much for them when they should be striving for greater maturity both as a person and as a follower of Christ.

The analogies to this guideline are endless. For example, how many of us as parents want to continue to dress our children when they should be dressing themselves? We expect a normal child to progress through the proper stages of development. At a certain age we want our children to dress themselves, to brush their own teeth and to feed themselves, and to not learn those behaviors would be unnatural. We teach our children about life and about God, and we expect them to grow under our loving guidance. We expect them to grow to maturity through various age appropriate stages. In fact, we become concerned if a child is not doing what is normal for his or her age group. The same thing is true in spiritual matters. We desire individuals to become mature disciples who are dependent on God. For us to create dependency in others so they do not learn to feed themselves spiritually, and in other ways for that matter, is a violation of this principle.

Steve Saint clearly recognized this first guideline when a Christian short-term mission team dealt with the Waodani tribe in Ecuador, South America. In relation to mission work, Saint states, "When in the name of Christian mission we do for the indigenous believers what they can do for themselves, we undermine the very Church that God has sent us to plant."[74] He goes on to say that our methods create an opposite result from what we want. He characterizes the result in this manner

> The people who were very independent realize that they cannot get along without the missionaries and resent being dependent. If the missionaries quit giving any goods or services that were being offered, the people, who have begun to see the service as their right, resent what is being taken from them.[75]

We teach others to do what they currently cannot do

We need to teach others to do missions and ministry that they are currently incapable of doing. As the commonly known adage goes, "give a man a fish and you feed him for a day, teach a man to fish and you feed him for a lifetime." We need to teach others to fish for themselves so that they do not become

---

[74] Steve Saint. *The Great Omission*. Seattle: YWAM Publishing. 2001. Pg. 58.
[75] Ibid. Pg. 53.

dependent upon us but upon God. He is the all-sufficient one, not us. This point could reveal a prideful attitude in us; we want others to depend on us. It makes us feel good that someone needs us. It meets an unfulfilled need in us. We all want to be appreciated by others. Yet, this is a prideful attitude. We debilitate others and keep them from reaching their full potential when we teach them to come to us to get answers to life's questions or to get their needs met. Those who had the greatest influence in our lives were those who mentored us and allowed us to mature under their guidance.

Willow Creek Pastor Bill Hybels, in a video explaining the results of a church-wide review, stated that their churches were not doing a good job of creating believers who could feed themselves spiritually from the Scriptures. In the church's report, *The Reveal,* the pastor said some of their methods created believers who were dependent on church programs and others for spiritual nourishment. Such believers became dependent on others and eventually created problems in the church because they were spiritual infants who needed constant care. The spiritual development toward maturity for those dependent believers was hindered along the way. This is a real problem with our consumer Christianity. Believers are taught to be consumers and not producers. At least Hybels and his leaders had the maturity to take a serious look at the results of their ministry efforts.[76] Creating disciples who can

[76] www.revealnow.com/story.asp?storyid=49

spiritually feed themselves is at the very heart of true discipleship.

What would happen if our disciples were to be persecuted for their faith and were not able to listen to the latest sermon on our church website? Or what if that disciple could not download something on his or her phone? What would happen if one of our disciples were persecuted and could not read the latest popular Christian book? Non-dependent disciples are resilient in the face of persecution. If we create disciples who are dependent on "things" then we have failed to create disciples who are dependent on God. Yes, God can use such things but what happens when they are not available? A mature believer will not only be able to feed himself or herself from the Scriptures but will also be able to spiritually mentor others so that those whom he or she mentors become spiritually mature.

Years ago a Christian couple told me that they were not able to survive spiritually without a group of support people around them. They could not survive without a local church body. My response was they could not be a cross-cultural missionary or be used by God to serve in an unchurched geographical area because they were not mature enough to survive without depending on others. Yes, we need the support of other believers but we must spiritually mature to the point of feeding ourselves directly from God's Word. Such non-dependent servants must know how to commune with God and feed themselves spiritually from the Scriptures. Church history, as well as modern examples, are replete with illustrations of missionaries who serve in difficult areas yet thrive spiritually by feeding themselves from God's Word. In other words, they have no support system but are mature spiritually. We should be blessed and ministered to by others but we should not be dependent on others for our spiritual growth. Paul did have a team of leaders around him in his later years of ministry. Paul was discipled by others but he grew to maturity because he took responsibility for his own personal growth. The basis of our life should be a direct relationship with God, who gives us spiritual nourishment.

The following example of teaching someone to do what he or she currently can not do has been duplicated countless times over the centuries. A missionary couple in the late 1990's was appointed to serve in rural Mexico with the International Mission Board. After completing a full year of language study, the couple moved to their chosen geographical region of service. The husband had no prior cross-cultural experience but was eager to learn. An older missionary couple, who was about to retire, befriended the new couple. The older missionary took the new missionary with him every day no matter where he went. As the older missionary went through his normal daily routine he would explain to the new missionary how and why he did things in a specific way. Many times, his activities were guided by culture more than anything else. At the end of one year of working with the older missionary, the new missionary was able to continue the Gospel efforts in that region because he had been discipled to be non-dependent. The older missionary retired while the work continued through the on-going efforts of the new missionary. The new missionary, who is now well-seasoned, has stated on many occasions that his success in ministry was due to the older missionary teaching him to do what he could not do.

Dependency and gifts

What is the difference between a gift that does not create dependency and a gift that does create dependency? Gifts that do not create dependency are those gifts that enhance, expand and broaden the mission efforts of the person(s) receiving the gift. For example, we give a gift such as a used car to someone who does not own a car. The car sounds like a good gift. Everyone should have a car, right? I know of a pastor who received such a gift. He was very thankful and humbled that someone would give him a car, especially one that he could not afford. But he later told me that he did not have enough money to purchase the gasoline to drive it, make the repairs when needed, or the other expenses associated with owning a car. I asked him what he did with the car after the visiting church team had returned home. He said, "The car sat outside my house for over a year because I didn't have the money to drive it. Then I eventually sold it so it wouldn't set in my front yard." This type of gift was a burden to the pastor and did not enhance, expand or broaden his ministry.

Correct gifts will elevate the ability of the person or group receiving the gift to greater ministry or mission activity. Around 2007 or so, I was asked by a church near Houston, Texas to be a co-teacher for part of their three-day church planting workshop in the Yucatán Peninsula in México. Their Spanish pastor was the main teacher, who taught a little more than half of the sessions, while I taught the other sessions. As the three-day workshop got started, I was blessed to meet so many great church leaders and believers. Before this experience, I had not visited a place where so many Mayan believers lived. I thoroughly enjoyed listening to them speak and hearing their language for the first time. I met one Mayan pastor who was crippled and walked with a crutch. It seems that he still had the use of one of his legs, while the other one hung limp. I was told that he was a highly respected pastor and leader among the Mayan believers. One afternoon while talking with a retired pastor, he mentioned the Mayan pastor. It seems that the retired pastor and his mission organization had given the Mayan pastor a small scooter as a ministry gift. Up to that point the Mayan pastor had been caring for two different churches, one in the valley and one in the mountain area. The Mayan pastor had a bicycle that he peddled with one leg up the hill in order to care for the members of that congregation in the mountains. That alone is amazing, peddling up the hill with only one good leg. But what is even more amazing, he also put his wife and small daughter on the bicycle. In other words, he peddled all three of them up the hill simply to make sure that group of people had a pastor. What commitment. I was told that the retired pastor and his organization purchased a small scooter for the Mayan pastor. The scooter also had a sidecar attached so the Mayan pastor could take his wife and daughter. The retired pastor told me that the Mayan pastor cried when he received the gift. He was overwhelmed by the thought that someone(s) would be so kind as to give him a gift that would allow him to enhance, expand, broaden the ministry to which God had called him. This is a great example of a non-dependent gift that blesses the one who receives it. The Mayan Pastor was able to afford the small amount of gasoline required to operate the scooter. Compared to the car in a previous example, the upkeep on the scooter was very manageable. Immediately upon receiving the gift, the Mayan pastor was not dependent on any outside source to use the gift to its fullest benefit. Non-dependent types of gifts are a hand-up not a hand-out to those who receive them. This is one such example.

Paul speaks of gifts that he had received, which were blessings that enhanced, expanded and broadened his ministry. He writes the following,

> You yourselves also know, Philippians, that at the first preaching of the Gospel, after I left Macedonia, no church shared with me in the matter of giving and receiving but you alone; for even in Thessalonica you sent a gift more than once for my needs. Not that I seek the gift itself,

> but I seek for the profit which increases to your account. But I have received everything in full and have an abundance; I am amply supplied, having received from Epaphroditus what you have sent, a fragrant aroma, an acceptable sacrifice, well pleasing to God. And my God will supply all your needs according to His riches in glory in Christ Jesus. Now to our God and Father be the glory forever and ever. Amen.[77]

Paul expresses his gratefulness to the church for sending him gifts on several different occasions. Reading from the passage, we can see that their gift did not make Paul dependent on the Philippian church. They were partners together.

Dependency summarized

Jesus stated the principle of creating disciples and not dependents this way, "Go therefore and make disciples of all the nations, baptizing them in the name of the Father and the Son and the Holy Spirit, teaching them to observe all that I commanded you; and lo, I am with you always, even to the end of the age."[78] Jesus said, "Teach them to observe all that I commanded you." Those who are being taught are expected to "observe" what they are taught. Personal responsibility is understood in this verse. Paul's

[77] Philippians 4:15-19
[78] Matthew 28:18-20

understanding of the principle of non-dependency is expressed in his letter to Timothy, "All Scripture is inspired by God and profitable for teaching, for reproof, for correction, for training in righteousness; so that the man of God may be adequate, equipped for every good work."[79]

If we are to develop mature reproducing believers and future leaders, we must avoid the trappings of dependency. David understood the process of maturity and the issues of non-dependency when he wrote the following words, "Your commandments make me wiser than my enemies, for they are ever mine. I have more insight than all my teachers, for your testimonies are my meditation. I understand more than the aged, because I have observed your precepts."[80]

[79] 2 Timothy 3:16-17
[80] Psalms 119:98-100

Key Concepts . . . .

- We do not do for others what they can already do for themselves.
- Dependency enervates, which means to deprive of force or strength and to destroy the vigor of something.
- Some of the methods we use in missions and ministry actually create an environment that stifles growth and harms our long-term efforts.
- Dependency handicaps and hinders the process of spiritual maturation by creating a welfare mentality.
- We should teach all believers to invest in their own spiritual development. To not expect such spiritual commitment is to allow others to remain undisciplined in their own maturation.
- We to teach others to do what they currently cannot do.
- Gifts that do not create dependency are those gifts that enhance, expand and broaden the mission efforts of the person(s) receiving the gift.
- Creating disciples who can spiritually feed themselves is at the very heart of true discipleship.
- If we create disciples who are dependent on "things" then we have failed to create disciples who are dependent on God.

¿-? Questions to consider . . . .

1. What in this chapter has challenged you?

2. After reading this chapter, how has your understanding of this principle changed?

3. In what ways might you be creating or allowing dependency in your discipling relationships?

4. What changes might you need to make in your ministry or mission efforts to avoid dependency?

5. In what areas of your life might you be dependent on others when you should take steps toward maturity and dependence on God?

6. What opportunities do you have in the near future to share the truths of this chapter with others?

Indigeneity

Defined

The word indigenous, in a general sense, means "native" or "originating in and characteristic of a particular region or country."[81] When referring to ministry and missions, indigenous pertains to what is native to or is characteristic of a people group or population segment. Every people group or population segment has distinguishable characteristics that make it recognizable from other people groups or population segments.

In relation to what is native to or is characteristic of a people group or population segment, we cannot live without culture. We are born into it and will die with it. The term "culture" is

> all the learned behavior, which is socially

[81] https://www.dictionary.com/browse/indigenous?s=t

> acquired, that is, the material and a non-material traits, which are passed on from one generation to another. They are both transmittable and accumulative, and they are cultural in the sense that they are transmitted by the society, not by genes.[82]

Missionary Eugene Nida also states

> Culture is a way of behavior, thinking, and reacting, but we do not see culture. We see manifestations of culture in particular objects (things made or used by people) and actions (what people do or say).[83]

God works through culture to communicate to us. This is reiterated by Anthony Conner who states, "All communication takes place within the context of culture."[84] God has chosen to speak to us in cultural contexts.

---

[82] Eugene Nida. *Customs and Cultures: Anthropology for Christian Missions.* William Carey Library Pub; 2 edition (June 1975). Pg. 28.
[83] Ibid.
[84] Anthony L. Conner. *An Oral Strategy for Training Leaders Among the Aztec Indians.* Doctor of Ministry Thesis Proposal Submitted to Liberty Baptist Theological Seminary in Partial Fulfillment of the Requirements for the Degree. November 2012.

The Yao Project

The Gospel will never reach its full expression unless it is allowed to be indigenous to a culture. When we expect others to become like us, an outside culture, we have violated the principle of Indigeneity. This is clearly seen in The Yao Project,[85] which was an evangelistic effort specifically designed to reach the Yao people group in Africa.

Several generations prior to the project, the Yao had rejected the Gospel because they were told, by a group of missionaries, that it was necessary to give up their Yao culture in order to become followers of Christ. To be a believer meant they could not be Yao and Christian at the same time. They had to choose one over the other. So, they became Muslims in order to retain their cultural heritage. Sometimes we forget how strong culture is to our self-identity and self-understanding. We cannot live without culture. It provides a daily structure and a method with which we interpret life and relationships.

---

[85] I first heard of the Yao Project in the late 1990's during a training session while serving as a missionary in Venezuela. Steve Evans was leading the training event. After his presentation I talked further with him because the various aspects of the Yao Project intrigued me. I wanted to him to teach me what he had learned. I later ordered a copy of the video and booklet from the International Mission Board who had produced the materials.

In the early 1990's, Steve Evans of the International Mission Board and other Great Commission Christians joined efforts to strategize and carry out a plan to present the Gospel in a culturally sensitive manner. S. Mpumila of the Mtambila Baptist Church and Alex Govati, who was the pastor of Nsomba Baptist Church, both "played an extremely important role in the recording of segments for the program, and in evaluating and testing."[86] The team's goal was to change the Yao people's perspective of the Gospel from one of strong resistance to one of openness and receptivity. In order to do that, they "produced Christian programs to the Yao Muslims through FEBA Radio from 1990 to the middle of 1992."[87] The missionary team visited "the chiefs and their people in their villages and recorded Yao stories and music."[88] The radio broadcasts featured Yao music and Yao individuals responding to various questions as an introduction to the Bible story for each particular broadcast. Every effort was made to demonstrate that one could be Yao and a believer in Jesus Christ at the same time.

Because of their efforts, negative Yao attitudes toward Christianity changed. After listening to the broadcasts and coming to realize that one could retain his or her

---

[86] Steve Evans – BACOMA General Secretary, Blantyre. 1.3.1991.
[87] Int Amos Phiri, Blantyre, 20.11.1997
[88] Hany Longwe. *Christians by Grace Baptists by Choice. A History of the Baptist Convention of Malawi.* Mzuni Press. 2013. Pg. 200.

cultural heritage and be a Christian, many Yao individuals became believers in Christ and new churches were started. One eyewitness recounts, "During this period many Yao people wrote to the program, and several people announced that they had trusted Jesus in the process."[89]

Cultural Insensitivity

Simply stated, the principle of looking at what is native or originating in and characteristic of a particular people group or population segment must not be overlooked. Many Christian workers who have dismissed this principle have made tremendous mistakes. Such mistakes hinder the Gospel from spreading quickly as Paul writes, "Finally, brethren, pray for us that the word of the Lord will spread rapidly and be glorified, just as it did also with you."[90]

When cultural insensitivity occurs on the part of the Christian worker, the Gospel message might not be received on the merits of the Gospel message itself but might be rejected simply based upon cultural insensitivity and offensiveness of the Christian worker. One only need to remember the Julie Andrew's movie titled "*Hawaii*,"[91] which is full of

[89] Int Amos Phiri, Blantyre, 20.11.1997

[90] 2 Thessalonians 3:1

[91] Abner Hale, a rigid and humorless New England

examples of insensitivity, cross-cultural misunderstanding and communication. When I was an adjunct missions professor teaching a Masters level class at a seminary, I showed parts of the movie as an illustration of what a misguided understanding of the phrase "making disciples of all people groups." This movie is filled with many violations of the N. I. R. principles.

All cultures and worldviews are tainted with and deeply affected by sin. There is no cultural worldview that is not crippled by it. Even our own culture, regardless of our origin, is contaminated by sin. Yet, having said that, not all aspects of culture and worldview are immoral or sinful. A believer must discern which parts of culture and or worldview violate biblical truths and which do not. If an aspect of culture and or worldview does not openly conflict with Scripture, a believer should not see it as a threat to the Gospel. But if an aspect of culture and or worldview does openly conflict with biblical teachings, a believer should and must wisely and lovingly engage the cultural practice with biblical truth. Many times engaging sinful cultural practices can be done by telling biblical stories that speak to

---

missionary, marries the beautiful Jerusha Bromley and takes her to the exotic island kingdom of Hawaii, intent on converting the natives. But the clash between the two cultures is too great and instead of understanding there comes tragedy. The movie was released in October of 1996. www.imdb.com/title/tt0060491

the cultural habit.

The Maijuna Tribe

A prime example of using Bible stories to change a harmful, cultural habit comes from the Maijuna tribe on the Amazon River near Iquitos, Peru. For over a year, missionary Brandon Carroll, along with Houston Pastors Ralph Clements and Gerald Coleman, used the chronological method of Bible storytelling to present the Gospel and disciple those who became believers. Brandon tells the story of how the Maijuna men had the custom of beating their wives. When various Bible stories were presented to the Maijuna men, who had become believers, they repented and asked their wives to forgive them. The cultural practice of wife beating was wisely and lovingly changed through telling Bible stories. It was the conviction of the Spirit of God that changed those men through the inspired narrative Scriptures. The men, who are believers, replaced the old cultural practice with new behaviors that honor Christ. Paul referred to the change that takes place in a believer when he wrote,

> Therefore if you have been raised up with Christ, keep seeking the things above, where Christ is, seated at the right hand of God. Set your mind on the things above, not on the things that are on earth. For you have died and your life is hidden with Christ in God. When Christ, who is our life,

> is revealed, then you also will be revealed with Him in glory. Therefore consider the members of your earthly body as dead to immorality, impurity, passion, evil desire, and greed, which amounts to idolatry. For it is because of these things that the wrath of God will come upon the sons of disobedience, and in them you also once walked, when you were living in them. But now you also, put them all aside: anger, wrath, malice, slander, and abusive speech from your mouth. Do not lie to one another, since you laid aside the old self with its evil practices, and have put on the new self who is being renewed to a true knowledge according to the image of the One who created him.[92]

Drunkenness, among the Maijuna, was also replaced with a biblical view though the same process of Bible storytelling. The men who had become believers became convicted of drunkenness after coming to the realization that God said it was a sin.[93] This cultural change took place after the new believers were presented with the truth of Scripture from Bible stories.

[92] Colossians 3:1-10
[93] Galatians 5:16-25

The Gospel and Culture

Anthropologist Paul Hiebert recognized our tendency to overlook this principle when he said, "as evangelicals we emphasize knowledge of the Bible, but rarely stop to examine the people in the cultures we serve."[94] When presenting the Gospel, a believer should take great care in making sure the message is clearly understood by the hearer in a manner that does not violate biblical truth but at the same time is appropriate to the listener's culture. Kraft expresses this thought effectively

> If we are to take the scriptural approach, we are to adapt ourselves and our presentation of God's message to the culture of the receiving people. If we demand that they become like us in order to be acceptable to God, we, like most of the early Christians (see Acts 15:1), have misrepresented God. We, the witnesses, are to make the cultural adjustments, not they, the potential respondents."[95]

When we desire to fulfill the Great Commission (Matthew 28:18-20; Mark 16:15; John 20:21; Luke 24:46-48; Acts 1:8) we must reach across existing barriers, whether cultural or other. The Great

---

[94] Paul Hiebert. *Anthropological Insights for Missionaries.* Grand Rapids: Baker Book House. 1985. Pg. 140

[95] Charles Kraft. *Anthropology for Christian Witness.* New York: Orbis Books. 2000. Pg 2.

Commission will never be carried out to its fullest extent if the Gospel is not allowed to permeate a culture. Paul communicated the principle of Indigeneity when he said,

> For though I am free from all men, I have made myself a slave to all, so that I may win more. To the Jews I became as a Jew, so that I might win Jews; to those who are under the Law, as under the Law though not being myself under the Law, so that I might win those who are under the Law; to those who are without law, as without law, though not being without the law of God but under the law of Christ, so that I might win those who are without law. To the weak I became weak, that I might win the weak; I have become all things to all men, so that I may by all means save some.[96]

Kraft makes a cogent point when he comments on 1 Corinthians 9:19-22

> From the beginning of Scripture, God has shown himself willing to work with people within their cultural frames of reference. He has always worked in terms of Jewish culture with Jews. Through Paul, he states what is illustrated in the book of Acts - that he wants to accept the Gentiles within their cultures also, without the

---

[96] 1 Corinthians 9:19-22

> necessity of their changing cultures in order to do things in a way that is acceptable to him.[97]

Jesus embodied this principle when he "became flesh and dwelt among us and we saw His glory, glory as of the only begotten from the Father, full of grace and truth."[98] Humanity saw God firsthand because Christ became flesh and dwelt among us in a God-ordained culture. He expressed the father's will from within the Jewish culture. In the similar manner people groups and population segments are able to know God when the Gospel is expressed through the medium of culture. Kraft goes on to say

> God seems to respect people's involvement in their cultures, even though this involvement entails practices that He does not endorse in any ultimate way. God's principles in this regard seem to be those articulated by Paul in 1 Corinthians 14:40 and 1 Corinthians 9:19-22. . . . The principles in 1 Corinthians 9:19-22 is that of the viability of any culture as a way of life and the usability of any culture for God's purposes.[99]

Kraft further comments

> Just as the apostle Paul sees each cultural matrix is usable for Christian witness, so we see God working in terms of Jewish culture to reach Jews

---

[97] Kraft. Pgs 1-2.
[98] John 1:14
[99] Kraft. Pgs 79.

> yet refusing to impose Jewish customs on Gentiles (Acts 15; Galatians). Instead, non-Jews are to come to God to relate to him in terms of their own cultural vehicles.[100]

The principle of Indigeneity is true even in our country of origin. Within our country of origin there are many subcultures to which we must adapt our communication methods to express the full message of the Gospel. However there are many who are concerned that we are somehow changing the Gospel message when we adapt communication methods in order to better engage the hearer. This is not true. The Gospel is very clear even when communicated in culturally appropriate ways. The power of the message is the Gospel. It must be communicated in such a way that those who hear understand it.

A fisherman has many options when catching fish. A hook is one option and a net is another. The manner in which a fisherman presents the hook changes depending on which type of fish he is seeking to catch. If the fisherman seeks to catch trout he presents the hook wrapped in colorful decorations. He uses a specific casting technique designed to present the hook in a manner in which the trout will best respond. It is easy to identify someone fishing for trout because of the distinct style of casting. If a fisherman seeks to catch catfish his methods are quite different. He drops the bait to the bottom the lake or

---

[100] Ibid. Pg. 449.

river. The presentation and the bait can be different in different contexts, but the Gospel hook remains.

When we adapt our communication methods in order to better engage the hearer, we are simply seeking to make sure the Gospel is expressed in a manner in which the hearer best understands the message. Kraft once again addresses the issue by making a cogent point

> We see culture is a vehicle usable by God, Satan, or human beings. We see no dichotomy between so-called Christian forms and cultural forms the forms God uses our cultural forms; none are sacred in and of themselves what we want is to be able to use cultural forms with Christian meanings. We see God wanting to reach each people group today in terms of their own culture, just as he sought in biblical times to reach Hebrews via Hebrew culture and Greeks via Greek culture. These are the cultures that were available to God in biblical times, so he used them. Each of them could have been called pagan when God first started using them. If God can use pagan Hebrew or pagan Greek cultures, he can use even pagan American culture or pagan African or Latin American cultures. . . . God was able to use even the cultural structures of that society for his purposes. I think the message here is that there is no culture that is unusable therefore, conversation happens within culture. The church happens within culture. Whatever changes happen as a result of Christianity are of

> the culture from within, transformation especially at the worldview level.[101]

The principle of Indigeneity is important to us because God has demonstrated that it is important to Him. The Gospel will never reach its full expression unless it is allowed to be indigenous to a culture. When we expect others to become like us, an outside culture, we have violated the principle of Indigeneity.

---

[101] Ibid. Pgs. 93-94.

Key Concepts . . . .

- The word indigenous, in a general sense, means "native" or "originating in and characteristic of a particular region or country."
- When referring to ministry and missions, indigenous pertains to what is native to or is characteristic of a people group or population segment.
- Every people group or population segment has peculiar and distinguishable characteristics that make it recognizable from other people groups or population segments.
- We cannot live without culture. We are born into it and will die with it.
- God works through culture to communicate to us.
- All cultures and worldviews are tainted with and deeply affected by sin. There is no cultural worldview that is not crippled by it.
- The Great Commission will never be carried out to its fullest extent if the Gospel is not allowed to permeate a culture.
- Jesus embodied this principle when he "became flesh and dwelt among us and we saw His glory, glory as of the only begotten from the Father, full of grace and truth." John 1:14
- The principle of Indigeneity is important to us because God has demonstrated that it is important to Him.
- The Gospel will never reach its full expression unless it is allowed to be indigenous to a culture.

¿-? Questions to consider . . . .

1. What in this chapter has challenged you?

2. After reading this chapter, how has your understanding of this principle changed?

3. What changes might you need to make in your ministry or mission efforts to be more indigenous to your cultural context while not changing biblical truth?

4. What opportunities do you have in the near future to share the truths of this chapter with others?

Reproducibility

Defined

Reproduction is a natural part of God's creation. God wants His creation to multiply. A great example of this principle is found in Genesis. God created Adam and Eve and told them to multiply and they did. From Adam and Eve we now have over 7.6 billion people on the face of the earth today at the time of this writing.[102] That number does not include all the people who have lived and died since God commanded Adam and Eve to multiply.

The same principle of reproducibility is true in missions. How we model ministry and missions is how others whom we influence will do ministry and missions. Paul wrote, "Be imitators of me, just as I

---

[102] www.worldometers.info/world-population is a website dedicated to calculating the current population of the world. The figure of 7.6 billion people was the number given at the time of this writing.

also am of Christ."[103] On two other occasions he stated, "I exhort you, be imitators of me"[104] and "Brethren, join in following my example."[105] His statement exemplifies the principles of reproducibility. In other words, the manner in which we model ministry and missions is exactly how those we disciple will do ministry and missions. We model what others duplicate. Those who follow us will replicate our style of leadership. There is an old saying that states, "more is caught than taught." This saying means that others learn more from our actions than from our words. When we invest in others they in turn learn to do ministry and missions the same way we do them. Over the years in many situations I learned the most from leaders who were poor model. I learned what not to do in ministry and missions from their poor examples. Yet, Paul makes his declarations in a positive sense when he states, "Be imitators of me, just as I also am of Christ."[106]

What we model is what others reproduce. This is a fundamental aspect of discipleship. A biblical example of this truth is expressed when Peter and John were arrested and brought before the Saddučees. Peter and John were told to not preach anymore in the name of Jesus. Luke writes, "Now as they observed the confidence of Peter and John and understood that they were uneducated and untrained

[103] 1 Corinthians 11:1
[104] 1 Corinthians 4:16
[105] Philippians 3:17
[106] 1 Corinthians 11:1

men, they were amazed, and began to recognize them as having been with Jesus."[107] Notice the phrase, "as having been with Jesus." They were modeling what Jesus had taught them.

Paul give us a tremendous example of four generations of disciples when he wrote, "The things which you have heard from me in the presence of many witnesses, entrust these to faithful men who will be able to teach others also."[108] This verse illustrates the principle of reproduction. All through the Bible, God's plan is multi-generational. Many times our view of God is based on our life, from birth to death. The Psalmist reminds us that God "has remembered His covenant forever, the word, which He commanded to a thousand generations."[109] We are also reminded of the horrific consequences, stretching to multiple generations, when we do not following the Lord, "yet He will by no means leave the guilty unpunished, visiting the iniquity of fathers on the children and on the grandchildren to the third and fourth generations.[110]

The Psalmist clearly expressed this truth by writing his view of each generation being taught about the Lord

> I will open my mouth in a parable . . . Which we have heard and known, and our fathers have told

---

[107] Acts 4:13
[108] 2 Timothy 2:2
[109] Psalm 105:8
[110] Exodus 34:7

> us. We will not conceal them from their children, but tell to the generation to come the praises of the Lord, and His strength and His wondrous works that He has done. . . . which He commanded our fathers that they should teach them to their children, that the generation to come might know, even the children yet to be born, that they may arise and tell them to their children, that they should put their confidence in God and not forget the works of God, but keep His commandments.[111]

Paul's Example

Consider the life of Paul. He had mentors and others who influenced him. Paul in turn became a believer who influenced others. Below is a short list of Paul's life and spiritual formation. When we apply the principle of reproducibility to ministry and missions we see its potential impact. The first example is a short list demonstrating a chain of reproducible influence from one generation to the next.

- Hellil,[112] a famous Jewish scholar,[113] influenced his grandson Gamaliel

---

[111] Psalm 78:2-4

[112] Also known as Hillel the Elder. "Hillel and his descendants established academies of learning and were the leaders of the Jewish community in the Land of Israel for several centuries. The Hillel dynasty

- Gamaliel[114] (mentioned in Acts 5:34-40) was a mentor to Paul - Acts 22:3
- Jesus was a mentor to the Disciples/Apostles - Luke 6:12-16
- The Disciples/Apostles were mentors to Barnabas - Acts 4:35-37
- Barnabas was also a mentor to Paul - Acts 9:26-27; 11:22-26
- Barnabas and Paul were mentors to John Mark - Acts 12:25; 15:39
- Barnabas was a cousin to John Mark – Colossians 4:10
- John Mark is the author of the Gospel that bears his name
- Paul was a mentor to Silas and Luke - Acts 15:40-41
- Luke wrote the Gospel account that bears his name and the book of Acts – Luke 1:1-4; Acts 1:1-2

---

ended with the death of Hillel II in 365 CE." Jewish Virtual Library. www.jewishvirtuallibrary.org/hillel-and-shammai

[113] "Hillel . . . was chosen by the Sanhedrin, the supreme Jewish Court, to serve as its President." Jewish Virtual Library. www.jewishvirtuallibrary.org/hillel-and-shammai

[114] "Son of Simon and grandson of Hillel: according to a tannaitic tradition (Shab.15a), he was their successor as nasi and first president of the Great Sanhedrin of Jerusalem." Jewish Encyclopedia. www.jewishencyclopedia.com/articles/6494-gamaliel-i

- Grandmother Lois and mother Eunice were mentors to Timothy - 2 Timothy 1:15
- Paul was a mentor to Timothy - Acts 16:1-3; 2 Timothy 2:2
- Timothy was a mentor to faithful men - 2 Timothy 2:2
- Faithful men were mentors to others - 2 Timothy 2:2
- Paul was mentor to:
  - Sopater of Berea, the son of Pyrrhus – Acts 20:4
  - Aristarchus from Macedonia – Acts 19:29
  - Secundus of the Thessalonians – Acts 20:4
  - Gaius of Derbe from Macedonia - Acts 19:29 and 20:4
  - Timothy – Acts 20:4; Romans 16:21
  - Tychicus – Acts 20:4
  - Trophimus of Asia - Acts 20:4
  - Lucius – Romans 16:21
  - Jason – Romans 16:21
  - Sosipater – Romans 16:21
  - Tertius – Romans 16:22
  - Gaius – Romans 16:23
  - Erastus – Romans 16:23
  - Quartus – Romans 16:23
- While under house arrest Paul was visited by:
  - Timothy – Colossians 1:1
  - Epaphras – Colossians 1:7-8
  - Onesimus – Colossians 4:9
  - Aristarchus – Colossians 4:10
  - Mark – Colossians 4:10
  - Luke – Colossians 4:14
  - Demas – Colossians 4:14

  - Tychicus – Ephesians 6:21
  - Epaphroditus – Philippians 2:25
  - Praetorian Guard – Philippians 1:13
- Paul sent others to do ministry
  - Tychius to Ephesus – Ephesians 6:21
  - Onesimus to Philemon – Philemon 12
  - Epaphroditus to Philippi – Philippians 2:25-30
  - Timothy to Philippi – Philippians 2:19
  - Artemas or Tychicus to Titus – Titus 3:12

This is only a list of those who were connected to Paul. This is a simplified list but true nonetheless. We could take Barnabas or other leaders from the Bible and create a list of all the people each one influenced. A study of the life of Paul from his conversion to the end of his life reveals a number of interesting facts.

First, he began to preach the Gospel shortly after believing in Jesus. He boldly proclaimed that Jesus was the Christ in an effort to convince his countrymen. There were other believers in the geographical area but he seemed to be refuting the Jews singlehandedly.[115] Paul had been changed by God and now was defending what he once persecuted. He was a man on a mission to proclaim the truth that Jesus was God's Christ. It appears that he went about this task independently after his conversion.

Second, after a long break of around 14 years,

[115] Acts 9:22 and following

Barnabas seeks him out and brings him to Antioch. In that city they both had a fruitful ministry. Paul,

one person, became two people, Paul and Barnabas.[116]

Third, in Acts 13 the Holy Spirit directs the Antioch church to lay hands on Paul and Barnabas to be commissioned as missionaries. They took John Mark with them. The group is growing. One has now become three.

Fourth, the pattern of multiplying disciples continued. By the end of Paul's life there is a list of no less than 24 names of other believers with whom Paul had influenced. Look at the list above. One person became 24 people and in turn those 24 people influenced others and multiplied into countless others. Paul's life is a great example of this principle in action.

Other Examples

There are many contemporary examples of the principle of reproducibility. We must ask ourselves the question, *"what type of Christ follower will be produced if we continue to do what we are currently doing?"* Beginning with the end in mind is a great benefit when considering long-term missions and or

[116] Acts 11:25-26

ministry impact. While serving as a missionary in Venezuela in the late 1990's, I was trained by the International Mission Board to begin with the end in mind or to end–vision (not en-vision) all of our mission efforts. We wrote a multi-year and multi-faceted master plan to guide our strategic focused Gospel efforts. Such a tool was very effective in keeping us on course to accomplish what we knew God wanted. As we used the strategy plan, we equipped national leaders and started 15 churches in 18 months using reproducible methods.

In 2002-2003 I served as a professor at the Seminario Teológico Bautista de México located in Lomas Verdes area of Satélite in Mexico City. During my time there I was part of a small academic committee led by Dr. Russell Harrington, the serving Academic Dean and missionary with the International Mission Board. The academic committee evaluated the curriculum and the student outcomes for each of the four years of study. The main question the committee sought to answer was, "at the end of the first (second, etc.) year of study, what do we want the student to know and to be able to do?" In other words, " what do we want them to reproduce?" We evaluated all four years of theological study based on how we answered that one question. The end result was a four-year curriculum that was more focused on equipping ministers who were better able to meet the challenges of the urban context. We focused the curriculum on being able to produce the same student outcomes each year of the study. We focused on reproducibility.

If we begin with the end in mind we will do a better job with the principle of reproducibility. Knowing what we want our final outcomes to be will determine how we begin. This is an important principle. We are failing if we do not understand and use this principle. Too many times in our mission and ministry efforts we model the wrong example. We should base our missions and ministry efforts on what we know to be the correct end result. As we invest our lives into the lives of others, we need to be cognizant of the next generation and the type of disciple we leave behind. Even though the concept of beginning with the end in mind had been around for quite some time, Steven Covey made it famous in his book, *Seven Habits of Highly Effective People*. Here is how Covey states the idea,

> Habit 2 is based on imagination--the ability to envision in your mind what you cannot at present see with your eyes. It is based on the principle that all things are created twice. There is a mental (first) creation, and a physical (second) creation. The physical creation follows the mental, just as a building follows a blueprint. . . . Begin with the End in Mind means to begin each day, task, or project with a clear vision of your desired direction and destination.[117]

Too many times we model the wrong example in our

---

117 www.stephencovey.com/7habits/7habitshabit2.php

mission and ministry efforts. We should base our missions and ministry efforts on what we know to be the correct end result. We should follow Paul's advice when he said, "be imitators of me, just as I also am of Christ."[118]

[118] 1 Corinthians 11:1

Key Concepts . . . .

- Reproduction is a natural part of God's creation. God wants His creation to multiply.
- We model what others duplicate.
- How we model ministry and missions is how others whom we influence will do ministry and missions.
- 2 Timothy 2:2 list four generations of discipleship.
- God's plan is multi-generational.
- Paul was mentored by other leaders.
- At the end of Paul's life, there were at least 24 leaders he had influenced.
- Paul modeled for others the way ministry and missions should be accomplished.
- Paul stated, "be imitators of me, just as I also am of Christ."[119]
- If we begin with the end in mind we will do a better job with the principle of reproducibility.
- We can see the progression of the principle of reproducibility in the life of Paul based on the list provided previously.

[119] 1 Corinthians 11:1

¿-? Questions to consider . . . .

1. After reading this chapter, how has your understanding of this principle changed?

2. In what ways might you include more reproducible methods in your discipling relationships?

3. When you begin with the end in mind and rethink your discipling relationships, what type of disciple will you be producing?

4. As you consider your spiritual journey, what have you learned from those who have invested in your life?

5. What opportunities do you have in the near future to share this truth with others?

Principles Applied

Each one of the following examples are given with the intention to clarify further how the three-missiological principles function together. The examples given are not intended to reference any specific church or individual but simply are offered as a better explanation of the truth of the N. I. R. Principles and how each one applies to real mission and ministry activities.

Example 1

A catastrophic flood took place in the central coastal region of Venezuela in December 1999. While we served as missionaries along the northern coast of Venezuela, we responded as best we could to the horrific humanitarian needs. All of the basic necessities of life were in short demand. One of the local elementary schools allowed us to host a hygiene class, which covered food preparation, proper bathing and hand washing, keeping cuts and scraps from being infected, as well as how to clean food utensils, bathrooms and kitchens. A female nurse on our team led the hygiene class and gave a Gospel presentation at the end. We gave a hygiene packet to each lady before leaving the classroom. The items of the hygiene packet were briefly discussed and the women were told which local stores sold each item. At the conclusion of the class, each lady knew how to properly protect her family from unwanted infections and sickness in a disaster area, as well as understood how to use each item in the hygiene packet and where to go to purchase more supplies. This was both a Great Commission and Great Commandment event. The Gospel was shared and human needs were met. Several ladies responded to the Gospel message, and their contact information was given to the pastor of the local church with whom we worked.

Example 2

A visiting church planned a trip to work with a host church in a large city in south central area of a bordering nation. The trip was planned down to every detail including the Vacation Bible School activities. The VBS materials used on the trip were the latest set of materials from a Christian publishing company. In addition to the VBS kit materials, the visiting church had made their own skit props and extra items to teach the lessons. Their teachers taught all the lessons using their VBS materials. After the VBS had ended, all of the teaching materials were given to the host church. The visiting church traveled over 20 hours one way to serve the host church with a sincere heart and pure motives. Everyone seemed happy and blessed by the experience.

Based on the N. I. R. principles, the following observations can be made. First, the sincerity with which the visiting church went to serve is commendable. Their motives were pure. They sought to help the host church and paid for their own expenses while on the trip. The visiting church genuinely saw their efforts as a gift to God and to his Kingdom expansion so that others might hear the Gospel. Second, the unintended attitude that was communicated by the visiting church was they alone understood how best to prepare and teach a VBS. Such was not the message they wanted to communicate to the host church but it was nonetheless implied. Third, there are several options, which could have been utilized to produce a longer lasting result from the visiting church's efforts. Remember the Steve Saint quote? "When in the name of Christian mission we do for the indigenous believers what they can do for themselves, we undermine the very Church that God has sent us to plant."[120]

Here are several ways that the wrong message was communicated through the methods used.

- By bringing all the materials for the VBS, the

---

[120] Steve Saint. *The Great Omission*. Seattle: YWAM Publishing. 2001. Pg. 58.

visiting church team communicated that the indigenous materials of the host church were not acceptable to do the VBS correctly. Only those materials, which were printed and purchased as that year's theme from the local Christian bookstore, were acceptable. Materials that the host church could provide were not adequate.

- By teaching all the classes, they communicated that only their teachers were capable of teaching each lesson and the host church teachers were unable to teach the lessons.
- By doing the whole VBS, the church communicated to the host church that there was not plan in place to have the host church learn to do the VBS on their own.

Here are several options that would follow N.I.R. Principles.

- Purchase the VBS materials in the local stores of the community where the host church resided. This would allow the host church to find teaching materials that are indigenous to their normal context. This also would communicate that the host church could prepare adequately for their own VBS by using what is available to them. Not every community lives in a part of the world with a local Christian bookstore or can purchase materials from an internet site.
- By purchasing their own materials in local stores, a host church with less resources is not dependent upon outside resources and would not need to wait until someone brings them appropriate

materials. They already have the appropriate materials they need in their own context.

- By purchasing their own materials in local stores, the host church is able to produce and reproduce their own supplies for each Gospel effort.
- Instead of teaching all the classes for the host church, the visiting church could take at least one of several options:
  - Co-teach the classes with a one-to-one approach. One teacher from the visiting church could teach along side one teacher from the host church to accomplish their responsibilities for the day as a team.
  - The host church teacher takes the lead and the visiting teacher serves as the assistant. The host teacher not only knows the language better in a cross-cultural context but also the worldview of the target group
  - Host a pre-VBS teacher workshop led by the visiting church. This would allow the host church teachers to learn the lesson plans, the crafts, the songs, etc. in order for them to teach their own VBS.

Example 3

Consider an example from the life of a missionary in Africa. The way in which we influence others is the way in which we should expect those we influence to imitate our actions. Some years ago a cross-cultural missionary told me that during his first term in Africa he had trained six men to start six new churches in communities that had no Gospel witness. Those six men started six churches while he served as their mentor. They met together once a week for over a year. The missionary taught the six men everything he knew about starting new churches. Before he returned to the United States for furlough, he asked each man to select one person he could train and together both of them would work to start a new church in one of the surrounding villages during the missionary's absence. The missionary left for the United States believing that he had effectively equipped six church planters who were going to select six other men and start six new churches in his absence. It sounded like a great plan because he could return to Africa and find 12 churches.

A year later when the missionary returned after his furlough, he expected to find six new churches. Yet to his frustration he found that his six church planters had not started even one new church, much less six. When he asked the six men why there was not one new church, they replied, "We are not able to start new churches." The missionary was perplexed at their answer since he had taught them everything he knew about starting new churches. He asked them why they had not started a new church since he had personally taught them. The six men told him that they were not able because they did not have an overhead projector. The missionary asked what an overhead projector had to do with starting churches. Their reply is very enlightening when we consider the N. I. R. Principles. Since the missionary had modeled his church planting efforts by using an overhead projector, the six men believed that in order to start a church they must also have an overhead projector. Such technology was not indigenous to their way of life and way of learning.

All six men learned in the equipping process with the missionary that certain items were necessary to accomplish their specific mission objective of starting new churches. In their way of learning and thinking, when the missionary did not provide each man with an overhead projector they were incapable of planting a new church in the next village. The missionary unknowingly had modeled a method of learning that was neither indigenous to the culture nor reproducible. He had introduced a learning tool into his methodology that was dependent on outside resources. He had violated the Principle of Non-dependency. He deeply regretted his error because he realized he had taught them a method that was neither indigenous nor reproducible and had created dependency. The church planting efforts were halted for over a year because of this one mistake.

Here is a possible solution. Bible storytelling is a method the missionary could have used to train the six church planters. The missionary could have used a number of options within the Bible storytelling method. He could have taught them an evangelistic set of stories in order for the six church planters to share the message of salvation. The missionary could have used a set of stories for discipleship, which were followed by a set of stories that taught what a New

Testament church was like from the Book of Acts. Stories are easy to remember, easy to reproduce and easy to apply to the culture of the hearers. Storytelling is a method that fits all three N. I. R. principles and you don't need an overhead projector to use them.

Example 4

A church took a six-member team to another country for a mission and ministry trip. A variety of activities took place such as giving personal testimonies during a joint worship service with the host church, a special service in which 20+ individuals were baptized, local orphans received needed hygiene supplies, Bible classes were taught and the visiting team members prayer walked a local outdoor park while giving a Gospel presentation to several individuals. The trip was a mixture of both Great Commission and Great Commandment activities. Before returning home, the visiting team gave the host church pastor a new computer program so he could more easily study for weekly sermons and Bible studies. The pastor had a computer so this gift was a great help to him. In his country such computer programs were not available for purchase nor could he have afforded it. This gift was a great blessing not only to the pastor but to the local congregation. The pastor's sermons and Bible lessons were able to improved, and his church became healthier in every aspect. Great Commandment activities were accomplish while the

Gospel was share and the host church pastor received a gift that did not create dependency but allowed him and the church to be blessed.

Example 5

In the mid-1990's a missionary to Africa told me of one huge mistake that he had made during his first few years. It seems that he had been assigned to a particular tribal group and his missionary assignment was to start new churches. He worked diligently to learn the tribal language as well as the culture. He did what he knew to do so he built a four-walled wooden building in which to hold Sunday worship services and weekly Bible studies. Several churches from his home country came to Africa to help construct the building which was for them a "construction mission trip." The missionary told me that it was difficult to get tribal members to come to his worship services and weekly Bible studies. As we talked about his experience, he expressed his frustration with the difficulty of learning the language, the culture, and motivating the tribal people to attend the worship services and weekly Bibles studies. He had spent a lot of money, time and efforts with little results.

Here are a few options that could have been used.

- The small wooden frame building he built in order to hold worship services and Bible studies was not indigenous to the culture. He could have built a grass-roofed canopy because everyone in the tribe lived in a grass hut. Four-sided wooden buildings were not indigenous to the host culture. So, the tribe was reluctant to go inside the foreigner's strange building.

- It was customary for the elders of the tribe met under a large shade tree in the middle of the village to discuss tribal issues and make decisions. The missionary completely disregarded the culture context in which he found himself. He could have met with the elders and the tribe under the shade tree in order to be more culturally appropriate and model a reproducible method at the same time.
- The missionary addressed the tribe without seeking permission from the elders of the tribe. The missionary showed disrespect to the elders by not seeking their permission before attempting to teach the tribe. Very few individuals would go hear the missionary give his weekly talks for two reasons: First, the elders did not give their approval. When an individual went into the missionaries house (the church building) to hear him talk, that individual was disrespecting the elders who had not given their approval. Second, the small wooden building was strange to the tribal group.
- The tribal method of communication was conversational. When the missionary gave his "talks" each week, only he spoke and everyone listened. There was no dialog. The cultural method of communication was to have a

conversation with the tribal elders in which everyone in the tribe could listen. If the missionary had spoken to the elders first and sought their permission, the whole tribe would have listened and been more receptive to his message because he would have communicated in a more culturally acceptable method.

- The best way to communicate with the tribe was to tell stories. The missionary gave his weekly "talks" using an structured outline which is an inappropriate style of learning for people who cannot read or write. A point by point structured outline many times is not appropriate for individuals who can read and write on a basic level. The missionary did not take into consideration the culturally appropriate method of learning which was storytelling. Using an outline and being the only one who spoke during these gathering were both culturally inappropriate methods.
- In conclusion, a more appropriate N. I. R. approach might look something like this:
    - Spend time with the tribal elders and earn their trust while developing genuine relationships. Be patient while earning trust.
    - Set under the community shade tree and learn tribal customs and worldview. Learn how the tribe communicates with each other as well as develop your skill to communicate the same way. Learn the intricacies of how they view life and the spirit world. Forget the four-walled wooden building, it's not indigenous. A working knowledge of culture and worldview

are necessary in order to be effective in Great Commission and Great Commandment efforts.

- Use the "construction team volunteers" to develop new relationships with the tribe instead of constructing a building that the tribe will not accept culturally.
- Learn the stories that are important to the tribe. Develop a set of evangelistic Bible stories that communicate God's self-revelation to man and leads the tribe to salvation in Christ.

Example 6

In the spring of 2002, I traveled to the capital city of a European country to consider a leadership position within our former mission organization. During my trip I stayed in the homes of several missionaries. On Sunday morning, one of the missionaries took me to a new church that was started by the most prominent church located in the capital city. The new church was located in a suburb of the capital and was doing a great job of reaching the immigrants who were living in that area. The majority of the immigrants were from Central and South America, but there were other church members who were from the Baltic States. During the worship service that Sunday morning, the host missionary stated that the new church could not do certain activities without the permission of the mother church. I asked him to explain what he meant by the statement. He clarified that the mother church would not allow the new church to baptize its own members or to have Communion unless the lead Pastor from the mother church was present. The mother church also chose the Pastor of the new church.

This system of church planting kept the new church dependent on the mother church. Under this system of church planting, the new church would have a difficult time learning to be self-supporting, self-directing or self-propagating.[121] Self government, self-support, and self-propagation are three basic principles that explain healthy, strong churches. Self-government "means the local church is able to make its own decisions under the Lordship of Jesus Christ. The local body should never be under the control of

[121] The elementary principles, of all types of churches in general, can be seen in church planting and missiological principles. In the 1850's two missionaries named Henry Venn and Rufus Anderson identified three principles of a healthy indigenous church. These principles were used by Melvin Hodges in indigenous church planting. He promoted the principles of self-government, self-support and self-propagation. Other church planters have restated these three principles for many decades. They are readily considered part of the expected end-results, as not only house churches are planted and developed but as other types of churches are planted and developed as well. Melvin L. Hodges. *The Indigenous Church*. Gospel Publishing House. 1953. Pgs. 17-81.

any foreign body."[122] Self-support refers to the local church bearing the burden for

> its own financial responsibilities through the contributions (tithes, offerings, gifts) of its members. This church does not develop dependence on outside sources but looks to itself, with the help of the Lord, to provide the resources needed as to personnel, materials, buildings, programs, etc.[123]

Self-propagation indicates that the local church "takes the Great Commission seriously and is devoted to the task of fulfilling it by winning souls and establishing churches."[124] A new church start must follow these three basic principles in order to be healthy. If fact, there are many established churches that do not exhibit all three principles.

The majority of existing churches are self-governing and self-supporting but they are not self-propagating. In such a condition, a church is plateaued and stagnant because it does not seek to share the Gospel with its own community. It is content to continue its weekly worship rituals without making an impact outside of the four walls of its building. Such

---

[122] Charles Brock. *Indigenous Church Planting*. Church Growth International. 1994. Pg 90.
[123] Daniel R. Sanchez, Ebbie Smith & Curtis E. Watke. *Starting Reproducing Congregations*. Church Starting Network. 2001. Pg. 111
[124] Ibid.

churches are many times unaware of their condition and like zombies – they are dead and don't know it.

Example 7

A Director, of a network of churches, was seeking to develop a long-term partnership with churches in the northwest United States. He made arrangements for several of his churches to travel to another state to help several small churches, which were a part of the newly emerging partnership. Both sides agreed on the calendar dates and that the Director would bring several churches to do a construction type project on their first trip. The Director and his churches paid their own travel, hotel and food costs. At the agreed upon date, the group arrived at the location to begin the construction project with the host churches. None of the host churches were present when the Director and his churches were ready to begin working on the first day. The host churches expected the Director and his churches to do the work for them. In other words, the host churches had not planned to participate in the actual construction project. They had planned to let the "outsiders" not only do the work for them but pay for all of the construction costs as well. The Director was unaware of this difference of opinion about the project. He would have never agreed to the project had he known the host churches were not going to participate.

There is a serious problem with this situation. But the problem can be easily remedied. The Director and his churches were not aware of the N. I. R. Principles. They would have handled the relationship differently had they been aware of the Principles. Here is an example of how the Principles can be applied. The Principle of Non-dependency states, *"We do not do for others what they can already do for themselves"* and *"we teach others to do what they currently cannot do."* As in Example 2, the could be two teams, one from each group. The two teams could work side-by-side to complete the task.

Example 8

A Baptist Convention in the United States formed a three-year partnership with the Baptist Convention in a South American nation. The United States convention sent a large number of teams on different occasions to help with various ministry projects among the Baptist churches in the South American nation. One such project was to help a small Baptist church in a large city on the Caribbean coast to construct a building in which to worship. The team from the visiting convention constructed the building with minimal help from the host church. Once the construction was completed, the visiting convention decided that there were to many mosquitos inside the building, so they installed windows. Once the windows were installed and closed in order to keep out the mosquitos, the visiting convention decided that it was too hot inside the building, so they installed an air conditioning system to cool the sanctuary. Of course, all of this was done with the best intentions – to help our brothers and sisters in the host church. The visiting convention returned home after a trip they believed had been very successful. A few months later the visiting convention received the monthly electric bill from the small host church.

Can you identify the issues in this story? This situation violates several principles. First, the visiting church was unknowingly creating dependency by giving those gifts, especially the costly air conditioners. The small host church could not afford the electric costs of the system and had to send the bill to the visiting church. This created dependency and not a healthy self-sufficient church. When we interact with other believers, churches or organizations we should always leave each one in a more healthy condition than before.

Second, it violates the indigenous principle. What was the situation before visiting team arrived and installed the windows and air conditioning? The members of the small host church were accustomed to living in that part of the world where the heat was very high and mosquitos were a problem. Obviously, they had deal with those issues long before the US team had arrived to help. When the visiting convention installed windows and air conditioning, they had not asked the members of the small church for permission to install those items. Even though the two gifts were given with the best of intentions, the small host church had neither asked for nor, more importantly, could afford to pay for the continual usage of the air conditioner. The host church believed the visiting church owned the air conditioners because they had paid for and installed them. Since the visiting church owned the church building and all of its contents, the visiting church should pay the monthly costs such as electricity.

Third, culturally the host church believed the air conditioning system was owned by the visiting church since they paid for everything and installed it was well. So, the host church sent the electric bill to the visiting church because they believed it was the visiting church's responsibility to pay for the expenses.

Example 9

Some time ago, I was told about a "mission" trip in which a team of church members traveled to another country to do a construction project. The volunteer team had scheduled five days in which to construct the four walls of the church building using concrete blocks. The volunteer team worked diligently and constructed the four walls of the church building in only four days, not five. The end goal of completing the project a day early became the focus of the trip. The volunteer team became more focused on completing the project in record time than in building relationships with the host church members. The volunteer team was excited and proud to have demonstrated such a work ethic to those who watched the team each day, which the host church members didn't think much about. The interaction with the members of the local church was minimal because the completion of the project was primary. The unwritten goal of the trip was more about the team members than about the local congregation. Once again, one aspect of the pattern that was used in Example 2 could be applied here. The host church could have selected a team to work with the visiting church team. They could have worked together while developing personal relationships.

Example 10

A missionary was working in a very remote area of the world and used the Jesus video to do evangelism in the surrounding tribal villages. Many missionaries have used this method with great success. The Jesus video is an excellent way to show the story of Christ in an indigenous language. The manner in which the missionary was using the video was interesting. His usual method of using the video was to load all of the video equipment into his truck and go to the next village. After arriving he would unload the truck, look for electricity, set up the screen, prepare the video player and projector as well as set up the sound. It's a lot of work but if someone gives his or her life to Christ then the effort is valuable.

But this method violates the N. I. R. principles. Here's how. The video equipment was not readily available in that remote context. It had to be brought in from the outside. In other words, no one in the village had video equipment. It's not indigenous. One must depend on an outside resource to use this method. Proper missiology seeks to use methods that are not dependent on outside resources. Also, this method is not reproducible by believers in the village because no one had video equipment and to be reproducible, additional video equipment would need to be brought to the village for trained believers to duplicate the evangelistic process.

When considering this method for the first village, what would be your strategy to evangelize the second village and beyond? A reproducible discipleship program would use the new believers from the first village to present the Gospel to the people in the second village. This means that the missionary would expect the believers from the first village to present the Gospel to the inhabitants of the second, the third, the fourth without him. A good question is this, "How would you have enough funds to purchase all of the equipment necessary for the new believers in each village to present the Jesus video to the next village?" Each new team of believers would need a set of equipment such as a truck, projector, video player, sound system, electric cords, screen, power supply, etc. Even if you didn't have a truck, you would need something to transport the equipment.

To use this method, you would need to purchase transportation, video projectors, video players, screens, sound systems and electric cords as well as many generators to supply electricity.

This is not a good method because it depends upon outside resources to purchase all of the equipment for each evangelistic team. There would be a lot of fundraising to purchase all the equipment necessary. This method is not indigenous to the culture of each village if no one in the village has a television. Yes, this method will draw a crowd but how many adjustments are necessary for others to hear the Gospel? This method is not reproducible. It creates a burden in fundraising in order to purchase the video equipment. It would be difficult to raise enough funds to purchase 20 or 30 sets of equipment as well as the vehicles necessary to transport the equipment. Even if you could use a boat to travel to each village, the average boat in that part of the world costs around $10,000 each.
Once again, we must consider other methods that are non-dependent, indigenous and reproducible if we are to be better stewards of the resources that God has given us. If we were to use the method just described in this example, what would be our strategy when the equipment breaks down or there is no electricity? There are other problems that might arise as well. In this strategy, evangelism would stop if the projector quite working. We must use methods that are non-dependent, indigenous and reproducible.

One possible solution that could be utilized is chronological Bible storytelling. This method is easily reproducible and each story will be interpreted through the cultural and worldview lenses of the hearer. This method does not need electricity, video equipment nor a vehicle to transport everything. The trained believer becomes a walking Bible, who can adapt to any context.

Example 11

A Baptist state convention of churches in the United States had a three year partnership with a Baptist convention of churches in a Latin American country. One trip each year to the host country consisted of over 200 medical doctors, nurses, optometrists and other health care professionals, which held health clinics in a variety of cities during the same week. Each year the medical professionals would offer free services as well as a Gospel witness to everyone who came to the health clinic. After several years of sending medical professionals to do health clinics, a study was conducted on the results of the multi-year effort. The findings of the study were interesting and revealed something that many did not expect. It seems that out of every 100 people who "prayed to receive Christ" there was only 1 person who could be found in the local church which had hosted the health clinic. What a disappointment. This means that after spending around 250,000 dollars for travel, hotel and food costs as well as all of the countless hours of effort to meet the health needs of selected communities, the evangelistic efforts were minimal. Yes, thank God for that 1 person who was following Christ a year later. But, one cultural characteristic probably influenced the outcome. In the host culture, it was customary to say "yes" to a request so that one would not hurt the feelings of the other person. How that cultural characteristic influenced the presentation of the Gospel at the health clinic was demonstrated in at least the following manner. The person receiving medical attention would culturally not want to hurt the feelings of the health staff, so that person would say "yes" to any request. The health staff would present the Gospel to everyone who came to the clinic. Individuals who were medically treated by the staff would politely say "yes" to the Gospel presentation because he or she did not want to hurt the feelings of the person who had come from another country to serve their community. Culturally the person was being polite in his or her response.

There were other issues involved in the results of the health clinics. The combining of Great Commandment activities with Great Commission efforts does not insure that there will be a reapable harvest. Sometimes an individual will "pray a sinners prayer" in order to make sure he or she receives the benefit of the Great Commandment activity. In the example above, communities were served, health needs were met and the Gospel was presented. Yes, Gospel seeds were sown. Yet, the vast amount of resources that were used for the yearly efforts produced minimal results. The ultimate goal is to see new disciples brought into the Kingdom. Once again as stated previously, we can feed the hungry, cloth the naked, visit those in prison but if individuals do not come to a

ABOUT THE AUTHOR

Darrell was a pastor in churches in Oklahoma and Texas. He and Karen served as missionaries for nine years with the International Mission Board in Costa Rica, Venezuela and Mexico City. They have five adult children, four of which are married with ten grandchildren. He served as the Executive Director for over 10 years of the San Felipe Baptist Association in Texas. He currently serves as the Executive Director of the San Antonio Baptist Association in Texas. He earned a Bachelor of Arts and a Bachelor of Science degrees from the Oklahoma Baptist University. He earned a Master of Divinity and a Doctor of Ministry degrees from the Southwestern Baptist Theological Seminary, where he also taught for 9 years as an Adjunct Missions Professor. Darrell is the former president of the Indigenous Amazon Ministries and continues to serve as a board member. He currently serves on the Board of Trustees at the Baptist University of the Americas. As a certified coach with the International Coaching Federation, Darrell actively coaches new church planters and other ministers. As a certified navigator with Church Unique organization, he helps churches rediscover God's unique design in obedience to the Great Commission. He is the President of The Matthew Affair, which is a non-profit organization who's mission is to teach and train the underserved.

The Matthew Affair
PO Box 100684
San Antonio, Texas 78201
thematthewaffair.com
a 501c3 non-profit organization

The purpose of our organization is to teach and to train underserved Christian pastors and church leaders around the world. It is estimated that the majority of Christian pastors around the world do not have any training in basic Christian theology. Without such training, many of these underserved pastors will believe and follow any number of false teachers and false doctrines. The majority of Christian pastors will never have the opportunity to receive vital preparation for ministry unless someone takes it to them. We are committed to investing in them.

The name "**Matthew**" was chosen because Christ's commission to His Church is found in the Gospel of Matthew 28:19-20, "go and make disciples of all nations, baptizing them in the name of the Father and of the Son and of the Holy Spirit, and teaching them to obey everything I have commanded you."

The word "**Affair**" was chosen because of its meaning. In the 1300's, the word "affair" meant "what one has to do." Affair has been defined as "anything to be done that requires action or effort." It is also "a person's responsibility, work or activity, which is done for a purpose. An "affair" is "something that must be attended to."

You can make a donation on our website. All proceeds from the sale of this book will be used by The Matthew Affair to achieve our primary purpose: to teach and train the underserved. The author of this book receives no financial compensation.

You can make a tax deductible donation at:
themattthewaffair.com

Made in USA - Kendallville, IN
23715_9780692160411
10.27.2023 1320